Leadership

The Ultimate Guide

Terry Melaugh

Disclaimer

This is an information guide. It is not intended as a substitute for legal or other professional services. While every effort has been made to make this guide accurate, it may contain typographical or content errors. The information expressed herein is the opinion of the author. The author and publisher shall have no responsibility or liability with respect to any loss or damaged caused, or alleged to be caused, by the information or the application of the information contained in this guide.

Also by Terry Melaugh

Get That Job - The Ultimate Guide

http://amzn.com/B00BV74E4E

How to Succeed at Work - The Ultimate Guide by
Terry Melaugh

http://www.amazon.co.uk/dp/B00CA9YOII

Table of Contents

Introduction

Introduction

Definition of leadership

The role of a leader is to inspire and lead others in the spirit of his vision. Leadership involves getting people to go further and achieve more than they would have done if left to their own devices. To do this a leader must create an environment where people can flourish. A leader must produce results through the efforts of others. To get others to perform to the best of their ability a leader must build respect and trust. Every member of his team must be willing and able to follow him.

A leader's role is to be forward thinking. A leader must plan for future events. He must set the direction for his team and then dictate the tempo of change. A leader must first of all have vision. He then needs to be able to articulate this vision to others. He must possess positive energy and enthusiasm in order to inspire and motivate others. He must have a winning attitude and seek positive outcomes.

Strategic leadership

Leaders exist at all levels of an organisation. At the top level the strategic leader directs the overall operation of the company. Strategic leaders are concerned with market strategy, competitor activity, growth, shareholder interests, acquisitions, mergers and the overall direction the company is taking. They set the overall purpose, vision and long term goals for the company. They are concerned with strategic thinking and planning. The strategic leader controls the company culture. This culture is often a reflection of the working environment that he personally prefers.

Operational leadership

Operational leaders are middle level leaders who will have a number of team leaders answering to them. Their role is to interpret the overall company objectives and come up with supporting divisional or departmental goals.

Team leadership

At the lower level of the organisation are team leaders. Team leaders are front line leaders. They lead teams directly involved in the services provided by the company. They are in charge of teams working in areas like production, quality control, customer services or sales.

For the sake of convenience this book will describe the role of the team leader. Most of the information provided can be applied to the role of the operational leader. Due to its unique nature, the role of strategic leadership is the subject of another book.

Chapter 1. The qualities of a leader

Intrinsic leadership qualities

Regardless of their function leaders seem to have certain intrinsic qualities. There has been a lot of debate in the past as to whether leaders were born with these qualities or whether others could learn to acquire them as well. It is generally accepted today that it is possible to train someone to acquire the characteristics of a successful leader. However it takes time and the acquisition of skills and experience. It also requires a desire and willingness to analyse personal behaviour and an ability to review and alter it. A leader must enhance his interpersonal skills in order to get the desired level of performance from each member of his team.

Vision

As a leader you must have vision and foresight. You must plan ahead. You must charter the way. You must provide your team with a sense of direction, meaning and purpose. Your team must clearly understand where they are, where they are going and how they intend to get there. They must understand how they can contribute to the journey.

Values

As a leader you must have a set of values. Your values are your moral compass. They will guide you to your ultimate destiny. Consider the things that are important to you. Consider the things that you will not compromise on. Begin by recognising your values. Then clarify them. Finally you must embed them into your behaviour. The decisions you make in life should be influenced by your core values and beliefs. If you don't stand for something you will fall for anything. All decision making ultimately comes down to values clarification.

Write down the ten most important values in your personal life and career. Typical values might be:

- I will be honest with myself and others.
- I will encourage and respect the views and contributions of others.
- I will treat everyone fairly and equally.
- I will recognise my own limitations.
- I will deliver on my promises.
- I will recognise and accept diversity in others.
- I will not tolerate prejudice in myself or others.
- I will aim to continually learn new things.
- I will always look for the good in others.
- I will listen carefully to what others are saying and show empathy.
- I will attempt to develop my team to the best of my ability.
- I will give something away every day.

Think about the behaviours that are most important to you. Think about the personal qualities that you would like to encourage in yourself and others. Think about how you want to be treated and how you want to treat others. Convey your values to each member of your team. They must understand the principles by which you are driven. They must know where you will not compromise.

Your values should be more important to you than your possessions. Losing your values will cost much more than losing your possessions.

Your values need to be more or less in harmony with those of your employer. There needs to be an alignment between your beliefs and values and the policies and change that you are expected to introduce and support.

Courage

A leader must have the courage to deal with conflict and other difficult situations. Leadership requires the courage to stand up for your values and beliefs. Courage is the strength to take the right course of action. Always strive to do what you feel is the right thing. Maintain your core values no matter what the circumstances.

Your own wants and needs should not override the needs of others. Look to find a balance between what is right for the organisation, what is right for your team and what is right for yourself. You should not need to look in the company rule book to know what is ethically and morally right and what is wrong.

Self-confidence

As a leader you must possess self-belief. You must be confident in your abilities. You must have emotional stability and self-assurance. You must be able to project this self-confidence onto others in order to build trust and belief in your capability as the leader of the group. This will enable you to gain the commitment of each member of your team.

Enthusiasm

Leaders tend to be charismatic. A leader must be passionate, enthusiastic and energetic in his role. He must be able to instil this enthusiasm in others. Enthusiasm is infectious and it is a key component in motivating others. A group will always pick up on the mood of their leader.

Self-discipline

Like all high performers a leader must possess an abundance of self-discipline. Discipline is all about putting in additional effort just when you feel like quitting. Discipline involves doing what needs to be done, regardless of whether you want to or not. Discipline involves overcoming setbacks and persevering when things are not going as expected. Discipline means sacrificing short term benefit to gain long term rewards. Discipline is what will give you an edge as a leader. By focusing on your long term goals you will be able to continue onwards when most other people have already turned back. Discipline is all about not quitting.

As a leader you must have a strong work ethic. You must be passionate about your core values and beliefs. You must always attempt to do your best. You must go beyond what is expected and what is required. You must set yourself apart. You must make a difference in everything you do and to everyone you meet.

Accountability

If you want to be a successful leader you must hold yourself accountable. You must accept responsibility for the work you supervise in your area. You must be accountable for the performance of your team. You must accept responsibility for any failures of your team. Commitment is a two way street. The members of your team will come to realise that you will not shift the blame onto them if things go wrong. By being personally accountable you will build trust and respect with your team.

Awareness

You must work on developing your self-awareness. You must be aware of your strengths and weaknesses. You must also be aware of the strengths and weaknesses of each member of your team. You must be aware of what motivates others. You must be aware of how exactly you can harness the energy of your team in order to support departmental goals. You must be aware of what each situation demands. The development of awareness leads to wisdom.

Watch how successful people get results by interacting with others. Watch how others fail to get the results they wanted. Note the difference. Learn from your observations.

Integrity

Leadership demands character. Leaders must possess integrity in order to build trust with their team members. As a leader you must be authentic and genuine. You must be honest and open with others. You must be authentic and straight forward. You must be true to yourself and to your word. You must practise what you preach. You must be 100% reliable. You cannot say one thing and do another. You must do as you say and say as you do. Do not pay lip service to your ideals. Honour your commitments. Always check resources before making a commitment. Make sure that you know that you can deliver when promised. Do not offer excuses for unreliability.

You must treat people with respect. To be a successful leader you must make yourself available to your team. You must be consistent in your demands. You must communicate clearly with others. You must not gossip about others.

As a leader you must treat all of your subordinates in the same manner. You must show dignity and respect for others. You must exhibit patience when dealing with people. You must recognise their limits and seek to develop their potential. You must be loyal to your team. You must never divulge anything that you have been told in confidence. You must support your team with their concerns and represent their interests to senior management. All of these actions will help you build trust with your team.

You must respect the feelings and opinions of your team. You must be open to opposing viewpoints.

Decisive

Leaders must know how to make timely decisions after gathering the right information and consulting with interested parties. If you are unable to do this then you will hamper the effectiveness of your team.

Open minded approach

Leadership is not a dominion over others. You should not surround yourself with yes-men. You must be open-minded. You must be willing to listen to advice, feedback and suggestions. You should be as open to bad news as you are to good news. You should surround yourself with wise council and competent advisers. You must, however, be willing to make the final decision based on the available facts. You must recognise your current level of knowledge and be continually striving to learn more about your organisation, your team, your objectives and your role.

Humility

A leader should have humility. He should be aware of his own limitations. A leader should be willing to learn from others. If you win in a particular situation, make sure you win with grace. Acknowledge the contribution of others. Never indulge in bragging. Nothing will turn people off quicker.

Even if you know more than others on a single subject it does not make you superior to them. A leader must be prepared to listen when others are advising that he is taking the wrong path. People who are full of their own self importance do not take time to listen to others. If you do not listen to others you will learn little of value.

Chapter 2. The Functions of leadership

The role of the leader

The main role of a successful leader is to:

- Provide common objectives and goals for his team.
- Keep the team working together as a cohesive group.
- Look after the needs of each individual team member in order to gain optimum team performance.

There are a number of common functions that successful leaders must carry out, regardless of their role within an organisation.

Providing direction

A leader must provide the vision for the future. A leader must set the long term goals for his team. He must define their overall tasks. He must then set the short term objectives that will contribute towards achieving the longer term goals.

Initiating change

A leader must initiate action and facilitate change. A leader must be decisive. He must be an instigator. He must be a champion of causes. He must be proactive.

Achieving results

You must direct your team in order to achieve business goals and objectives. You must be results focused and teach your team to think likewise. Do not confuse activity with achievement. Concentrate on the ends, not the means. Results, not effort alone, bring success. A leader should constantly strive to find solutions to problems.

Making a positive difference

Your aim should be to make a positive difference to those around you. You should be able to make a difference in how people feel about their work. You should create an environment of trust, camaraderie and understanding. You should help people to enjoy their work.

Communication

A leader must use communication to build relationships with his team and others within the business. You must develop internal and external networks and partnerships in order to help achieve your goals. You must build trust through constructive working relationships. You must be able to influence and engage others.

You must develop excellent communication skills in order to be effective in your role as leader. Communication is the main tool that you will use to get results. Through communication you will get to know and understand the individual requirements of each member of your team. You must brief each team member on the reasons for and importance of their overall goals. You must explain their role in contributing towards the overall company objectives.

You must provide your team with regular updates on how the company is performing. You must indicate how their contributions have helped to achieve these results.

Encouraging participation

A leader must ask for ideas and suggestions from his team and his work colleagues in order to enhance the feeling of participation. As a leader you must value diversity. You must focus on collaboration rather than confrontation or competition. Common solutions will help others to buy into your proposals.

Building relationships

You must build and nurture relationships if you want to succeed. Trust is the cornerstone on which all relationships are built. As leader you must know how to develop and maintain trust with each member of your team and other co-workers.

Delegating

A leader must delegate most of the tasks that comes his way. Your role as a leader is not to carry out detailed tasks. That is the responsibility of your subordinates. You must delegate most of the work by instructing each team member on his individual tasks and responsibilities. You must define the acceptable standards of work. You must ensure that the tasks are clearly understood and that each team member is happy with his assignment.

Your role is to develop the skills and confidence of each team member by delegating to them progressively more challenging tasks.

Organising

A leader must organise individuals, resources and time in

order to achieve each objective in an efficient manner.

Controlling

As a team leader you will control or direct the output from the group. Your job is to keep everyone on track. You will set the tempo and define the acceptable standards of behaviour and performance. You will measure performance, provide feedback and let each member know if they are hitting their individual targets. You will have to prod and encourage others to help achieve the team goals. You will have to let individuals know if they need to improve their performance.

Coaching

One of the main functions of a leader is to coach others. New leaders must appreciate that they are no longer a team player. They are the team coach. Their function is to guide, motivate, support and encourage others to achieve common goals and objectives.

A leader must support each member of his team in their work. You must do this by instilling trust in each team member. You must listen to concerns and provide advice and guidance. You must provide feedback on performance and advice on how to improve it. Your job is no longer to do things for people, but to help them to do things for themselves. Your job as coach is to continually make small improvements to individual performance that collectively add up to big improvements on team performance. It's the little things that make the difference in the long run.

On the job coaching

You can spend ten minutes and show someone how to carry out a new task when delegating it to them. Start by doing some new aspect of the task and explaining what you are doing. Then ask them to do it while you talk them through it and remind them of the required steps. Finally get them to do it and talk you through it, while you correct anything that they have not yet grasped.

Motivating

A key role of leadership is motivation. You must be able to develop and encourage others. You must motivate each individual team member so that the group as a whole achieves its targets. Leadership is about managing the emotions of others in order to get the optimum performance from them. The way people feel influences the way they think and act. Emotions affect decision making, energy levels and behaviour.

Representing

As leader you represent the interests of your team to senior management. You will need to defend the group against attack from other departments and act on behalf of the group.

You must also represent the interests of the organisation to your team and others. You must champion any initiatives aimed at change. Your power and position require you to represent the company and support any policy as if it where your own.

The leader as role model

You should be aware that as a leader you will be expected to be a role model for your team. Others will watch and listen to the way you behave. They may model their behaviour on what you do and how you act. They will mirror your actions.

Removing barriers

A core part of a leader's responsibilities is to recognise and remove barriers to progress. A leader should be able to think outside the box in order to do this. You should not constrain your team with redundant procedures, paperwork, red tape and the need for you to sign off every little decision. You should also deal promptly with any problems or concerns that hamper progress. You should deal with any disagreements or conflict immediately.

Chapter 3. Leadership styles

There are a number of different leadership styles and it is possible for one individual leader to adapt more than one style depending on the prevailing circumstances.

Autocratic leadership style

Autocratic leaders retain complete command. It is a dictatorial method of command. They hold onto power. They make all the decisions. They want to remain in control. They issue instructions and expect orders to be obeyed. There is no consultation. There is little concern for the views and feelings of followers. The emphasis is on the task, not the individual. Ideas and input from the team are not welcome. There is a lack of trust and possibly respect between the team and the leader. There is no credit given to the team for results. There is a lack of motivation and loyalty. This type of leadership leads to absenteeism, stress-related problems and high turnover.

Historically this was the prevalent leadership style. It would still be recognised today in the military environment. Orders are issued with an implied threat of discipline or punishment if they are not followed to the letter.

Autocratic leadership has the advantage of guaranteeing quick decision making. A leader may decide to employ this style for short periods of time, such as in a crisis, where prompt corrective action is required to prevent losses. It may also be adapted when the leader is an expert in the area and so does not need the input from his team who are merely carrying out a supporting role. A leader may choose to use this style to address persistent under performance.

Laissez-faire leadership style

Here the leader takes a back seat and lets the team get on with their jobs. The team is allowed to make their own decisions and to follow their own path. The views and suggestions of the team are welcome. This leadership style will work if the team members are skilled, loyal and experienced.
This style of leadership can lead to a lack of direction and urgency. It can be counterproductive as team members feel that the leader is not setting the agenda or making timely and effective decisions.

A leader will employ this style on occasions to help develop individual members of his team by encouraging them to make their own decisions.

Democratic leadership style

Democratic leaders involve the members of their teams in the decision making process. However, the ultimate decision making power resides with the leader. This is a participative style of leadership. The leader listens to suggestions from team members and implements these if he feels that they will contribute to overall performance. This type of leadership improves morale and motivation levels. People are more likely to support working methods that they have been involved in developing. This style of leadership encourages thinking, creativity and ownership. It takes longer to reach decisions and there is a degree of uncertainty at the outset. This leadership style allows trust to be developed between the leader and his team.

Your leadership style

As a leader you should adapt the democratic leadership style most of the time. You will have to use the autocratic style and the laissez-faire styles at times. However these occasions will be limited and the approach will only be taken under certain circumstances.

Chapter 4. Behaviour and etiquette

Setting boundaries

As a leader you are no longer a member of the team. You have the responsibility of maintaining discipline. You must set clear boundaries. Your team must understand the boundaries and the consequences of either yourself or others crossing them. You must set clear standards for behaviour.

You must know where to draw the line. You must specify the rules. You must not allow infringements of these rules. The rules must apply to everyone in an equal manner if you are to maintain the cohesiveness and harmony of the team.

Punctuality

Insist on punctuality for meetings and attending work. Make sure that you re always punctual yourself. Turning up late for a meeting sends a clear message that you do not care about the person holding the meeting or the other attendants.

Politeness

Be polite with everyone you interact with at work, regardless of their station. Let your team know that you expect the same behaviour from them.

Profanity

Refrain from profanity at work and while on work

business, dinners or outings. Expect others to do the same. Swearing does not portray the right professional image.

E-mail etiquette

Do not send e-mails if you are angry or emotional. Do not write anything in an e-mail that you might later regret. If you have a problem with someone, wait until after you have calmed down, then arrange to meet them to discuss the issue. Once an e-mail is sent, the damage is done. There is no getting it back.

If you receive a negative e-mail from someone else, arrange to meet them face to face to discuss the difficulty.

Do not send or forward any jokes or inappropriate photographs by e-mail. Your employer has provided this facility for the purpose of work only. Insist that your team follow your guidelines on the use of e-mails.

Stick to facts

When holding conversations stick to the facts. Keep your opinions to yourself. Opinions alienate people who disagree with them. Unless someone specifically asks for an opinion, they never value it.

Never complain

Never complain. Complaining turns people off. Complainers seek to divert attention from their own inadequacies by pointing the finger of blame elsewhere. You should be a solution provider not a fault finder. If you have a problem with someone else's behaviour, either ignore it or address it tactfully with the person concerned in private. Do not complain about them to others. If you have a problem with a practice or procedure, then suggest a way of improving on it. Do not complain about it or you will develop a reputation as a whiner.

Never hold grudges

There will be times when you will be treated unfairly by others. There will be times when your proposals are defeated. There will be times when you are belittled by others in public. There will be times when you hear that others are talking about you behind your back. Tackle the issue directly with the person involved if you feel that you must do. However, never hold a grudge for someone because of what they have done or what you perceive that they have done. Grudges are emotionally, physically and mentally draining for those who carry them.

Holding grudges and the desire for revenge wastes time and productivity. It shifts focus from forward looking positive acts to backward looking negative feelings. The desire to get even is a form of self-pity. Do not carry your demons around with you. It is better to get angry at the time, vent your emotions and then move on. Channel your energy into outperforming the person who slighted you. That is the ultimate payback.

Learn to control your emotions

Learn to control any negative emotions in yourself. Learn to regulate your behaviour. Be aware of how you react in demanding or stressful situations where there is conflict. Practice remaining calm and not raising to the bait. Slow down if you begin to get angry and lose control. Count to ten before you speak. Remove yourself from the situation until you can calm down. Never make a situation worse by losing control of your own emotions. If you do, be prepared to apologise and make up for the wrong doing.

Chapter 5. Emotional Intelligence

Emotional intelligence reflects the ability to recognise and manage your own emotions as well as the emotions of others around you. The ability to communicate and to influence others is directly related to the level of a person's emotional intelligence. All leaders must be aware of the need for emotional intelligence when dealing with others. Understanding people and empathising with them reaps greater rewards than issuing commands while ignoring the input and feelings of others.

People are different and they respond differently to various methods of persuasion and motivation. If you are going to succeed then you need to take this into account when dealing with people. You must be aware of people's emotions when interacting with them. You must also be aware of your own emotions and be able to keep them in check.

Be aware of the emotions in others

You need to be constantly aware of the emotions in others. How are they reacting to you and with one another? Are they defensive or withdrawn? Are they outspoken or aggressive? Is their tone or language negative or doubtful? What is the expression on their faces? What does their body language tell you? What is their energy level when you make a suggestion? Are they enthusiastic, indifferent or lethargic? If you detect any signals that they are not fully committed to your proposals then you must ask about their feelings. Get them to voice their concerns. Encourage them to open up.

Be tactful

Be tactful in how you deal with problems, mistakes and issues. Do not rush in with your opinions. Ask others first how they feel about the situation. Often this is all you need to do. They do not always need you to tell them that they made an error. They will recognise a mistake themselves and suggest ways of avoiding it in future. Keep your council to yourself when you can. Avoid criticising others if you possibly can. It is better to lead by example than by admonishment.

Ask about feelings

Even when you are not issuing commands you should regularly ask your team members how they are getting on. Take a moment when walking past a team member to ask if everything is all right. Ask how they are feeling and how they are keeping. Ask if there are any problems. Ask if there is anything that you need to do to help them. This only takes a few moments, but it makes a world of difference. Do this at least once every day with every member of your team. If you want to build trust and respect then you must show genuine concern and support for the members of your team. You must be there for them when they need you most.

Deal with negative emotions

You must be able to recognise and deal with the signs of negative emotions in others. You must recognise the emotion, find the underlying cause and help the other person to alter their perspective.

Discomfort

People are sometimes uncomfortable about a situation without really understanding why. They become impatient, bored, uneasy and restless. If you detect these emotions in a member of your team you probably need to clarify their goals and the contribution that they are making.

Behaviour that prevents empathy and rapport

There are certain behavioural traits that you must avoid if you want to display empathy, build rapport and gain the trust of others.

Dominating or aggressive behaviour

Dominating or aggressive behaviour will prevent rapport building. Threatening subordinates with punishment, giving abrupt orders in a harsh tone, criticism, sarcasm, name calling and abusing are all counter-productive.

Manipulative behaviour

Withholding relevant information, coercing, interrogating and praising just to get a favour are all forms of manipulation which will prevent the building of rapport.

Denial

Avoiding an issue rather than dealing with it only leads to a greater problem further down the line.

Not listening properly

Not paying attention, failure to ask questions, interrupting, changing the subject, dismissing and ignoring are all barriers to building rapport.

Improper advice

Sometimes you just need to listen to people without adding your comments. The other person is just looking to off load, calm down or think through their own problem. They do not want untimely advice. They want to come to their own conclusions. When someone is obviously distressed it is human nature to want to help and provide advice. However this is not always the best course of action.

Offering advice when a person just wants to be listened to is also a barrier to building rapport. Challenging emotions views with logic will also have a negative effect.

Chapter 6. Developing your leadership skills

Take stock

Begin by taking stock of where you are in relationship to where you want to go. Analyse your strengths and weaknesses. Be honest with yourself. Ask friends and family to list your three greatest strengths and three things that you should work on. You may be surprised at what they tell you. Be prepared to accept their judgement. The secret of successful people is that they are self-aware and work to their strengths.

Take time once per month to review how you are developing as a leader. Consider what is working and what is not working so well. Be prepared to try something new.

Life-long learning

Perennial learning is critical for both you as leader and the members of your team. You cannot develop or progress without learning. Your future prosperity depends on learning. When you finish your formal learning at school, college or university the first thing you need to realise is that the learning has only just begun.

Methods of learning

You can learn by experiencing, reading, watching, listening, doing, discussing, studying, reflecting or travelling. You can learn by questioning. You can learn by taking notes. You can learn by visualizing. You can learn by keeping an open mind. You can learn by trial and error. You can learn by making mistakes. You can learn by failing. You can learn by reviewing your behaviour. You can learn by listening to advice and feedback. You can learn from criticism received, constructive or otherwise. There is no limit to the ways in which you can learn and develop.

Learn from every experience

You must endeavour to learn from every situation. Keep a log of your major daily encounters and review it every evening. Reflect on your performance. Think about how you responded to others and how you behaved. Think about what you said and what you could have said. Consider what you did well and what you could have done better. Think about what contributed to your goals. Consider the distractions and how you can avoid them in future.

Think about the consequences of your behaviour. Think about how others responded to you. Did you contribute to their sense of well being? Did you make their day a better one? Think about how you could have managed the situation better. What will you do different in future?

Learn from every experience. Learn from others. Learn from your mistakes, but also learn from your successes.

Learn from your failures

Not everything you attempt to do will succeed. This is not important. What is important is how you react to failure. The important thing to do is not to give up. Never submit to failure. You must learn from every failure and take an alternative course of action next time.

Learn from the mistakes and successes of others

Study how others behave. Look at what gets results for them. Look at what does not work for them. Listen to their advice. Take advantage of their experience.

Learn from everyone in your organisation

Spend time in every area of your organisation. Ask to shadow people in their jobs. Get to know how every department functions. Learn to see how your area of responsibility is viewed by other people and other areas. Get to know your internal customers and suppliers.

Work smarter

Concentrate on working smarter, not harder. Focus on results. Seek new solutions to old problems. Question each and every activity that does not lead to results. If a task has no importance, then it should be dropped.

Read

Read self-help books. Read leadership books. Read books on your area of expertise. Read professional journals.

Training courses

Attend training courses whenever you can. Do not simply rely on the company to provide your training. There are plenty of inexpensive short seminars or courses available if you take the time to look them up. Adult education is an industry in itself. A lot of evening courses are available at local technical colleges.

Be curious

Be curious about everything around you. Continue to ask questions and to study throughout your life. Feed your mind through reading.

Look for a role model

Identify other leaders with whom you can relate. Look at the qualities of others that you admire. Attempt to emulate these qualities in your behaviour.

Take the road less travelled

Be prepared to take the road less travelled. In fact go where there is no road and blaze your own trail. To reach your goals you must make choices and sacrifices. If there is no pain, there is no gain. Success is not covered by warranty. If you want to succeed then you must be willing to take calculated risks.

You must be prepared to leave your comfort zone and experience new challenges. A ship is safe when anchored in a harbour. But that is not what ships were built to do. It is not enough to follow the herd. You must set out on your own journey of discovery. You must follow your own path. You must be prepared to take risks if you are to achieve anything worthwhile.

Talk to a stranger every day

Initiate a conversation with a stranger every day. Take yourself out of your comfort zone. Most people stick to their circle of friends or colleagues at work. If you take the time to talk to someone new each day it will prepare you for those occasions when you have to interact with new customers, suppliers or other business acquaintances.

Believe the best is yet to come

While you should strive for satisfaction in what you do and what you have already achieved, you should always believe that the best is yet to come. Do not accept that you have arrived at your destination. Always believe that you can do better. Your attitude should be that you can achieve more and you can provide more. What's more, you can inspire others to achieve more. The competition is not standing still. Better methods of doing things are being developed daily. You should continually quest for improved ways of finding solutions.

Practise makes perfection

Continually practise your skills in order to improve them. There is very little that cannot be improved in this way.

Be creative

You must be prepared to think and act creatively. Engage your mind. You must consider new ideas and new ways of doing things. Do not rely on the tried and trusted methods as these will one day become outmoded and obsolete. Everything changes and you must change also if you are not to be left behind.

Be yourself

You must evolve your own set of values and principles and be true to them at all times. Your behaviour patterns will reflect your values. Your core beliefs are what differentiate you from the masses. Stick to your values and beliefs. Be yourself.

Be flexible to change

If you want to learn you need to be open minded and flexible to change. Better ways of doing things are continuously being evolved. It is not enough to apply the techniques that worked in the past. You must be open to new ideas and methods.

Be generous

Give something back every day. You will become richer in the process. Give your help. Give your insight. Give your advice. Give a listening ear. Give empathy. Give a smile. Give praise. Give a word of encouragement. Give a lending hand. Give a pat on the back. Give to charity. Give to those who cannot afford to give it back.

Once you have given, forget it. Remember what you have received.

Measure your performance

Do not rely on your boss to measure your performance once per year. Measure it yourself each and every day. Set your standards high and measure how you perform against them. You should have at least 6 or 7 key performance indicators (KPIs) that you want to measure. Listening might be one of them, motivating might be another. You should pick one of these KPIs each week and work actively on improving it. So for a whole week you can work on your listening skills. The next week you can concentrate on improving your motivational skills.

Maintain your equilibrium

Keep your life in balance. Maintain you work-life balance. Do not over commit. Take time for the things that are important to you. Allow yourself some quiet time each day where you can relax and reflect on your sense of well being. Allow yourself a reward each week where you take time out to enjoy an event with your family and friends. Have a friend and confidant with whom you can discuss issues that are important to you.

Chapter 7. Goal setting

Why Set Goals?

Goal setting is the fundamental requirement of leadership. A leader must have vision. In order to lead others he must first know the destination. He must then charter the course. Only then can he contemplate gathering a crew and embarking on the journey.

Successful athletes and leaders set personal goals and work relentlessly to achieve them. Goals give direction and help establish priorities. Goals clarify aspirations. Goals set a challenge for your team. Goals help the team to keep score and measure progress. Goals create a sense of urgency and purpose. Goals help to bring out the best in people. Goals focus minds and galvanise a team to work for a common purpose. Goals create a sense of cohesion.

Leaders must think ahead. They must strive to introduce change and better methods of operation. They must evaluate options and select the direction their team must take. The best way to do this is to set the overall goals for their area of responsibility.

Over 90% of the people who set goals achieve all or most of their objectives.

The importance of goal setting

In order to be a successful leader you must set goals. You must know exactly what you want. You can then work out the best way of getting it. All of your future actions can then be prioritised so that you reach these goals as quickly as possible.

Goals give you direction. They give you a sense of purpose. They help you focus. Goals provide you with a clear vision. Goals help us to think ahead. Goals help you to distinguish between the important issues and tasks that should be dropped or delegated.

Build your dreams

You should have an overall purpose to your life. Your long term goals need to be aligned to your personal values. Consider the type of leader you aspire to be. Think about your unique skills and talents. Think about the qualities you admire in others. Think about your heroes from fiction, history, politics or mythology.

Your goals must excite and inspire you. Set goals that you can be passionate about. The best way to lead others is through enthusiasm and passion for your cause. Once you have a vision it should drive all of your future endeavours. Your long term goals should challenge you to develop and grow as a person.

There is no limit

What do you want from your life? You can achieve anything if you set your mind to it. The future is yours alone. There is no limit to what you can do. You are surrounded by opportunities. You just need to recognise them. If you believe in yourself and you are willing to persevere there is nothing you cannot achieve. All things are possible. The only limit is your level of self-belief. Self-limiting beliefs are the only thing that can hold you back. You control your destiny. You are in charge. You control your thinking. You can win if you believe in yourself and you commit to the journey. Where there is a will, there is a way.

Set your ultimate career goal

Goals help you to bridge the gap between where you are now and where you want to be. Your long term goals will set your overall perspective and direction. Begin by taking stock of your current situation. Look at your position, your earnings and your recent appraisals. Be honest with yourself. What are your strengths? How can you best utilise them? What are your weaknesses? What do you need to do to improve on these areas of weakness?

Now decide what you want to achieve from your career. What is your ultimate destination? What level of responsibility and accountability are you willing to take on? Create a mental image of what you want to be. Consider the benefits that will accrue. What kind of person do you ultimately want to be?

Perhaps you want to be global sales director in your current company. Maybe you want to set up your own business. You might want to retire early. Write down exactly what you want to achieve. Write down the reasons for this ultimate career goal. Write down the benefits that will accrue from this success. Imagine how it will feel when you reach your goal. Picture yourself as the successful person you want to be. Now take a few minutes to imagine what it will feel like.

Setting medium and short term goals

Next set intermittent or shorter term goals that will help move you towards your longer term goals. These are the milestones that you must reach along the way. Write these goals down also. If you want to be the global sales director you may need to set two intermittent goals. If your current job is regional sales manager, your first intermittent goal would be to become UK Sales Manager. Your second goal would be to become European Sales Director.

You then take your first goal and break this down to a three year plan. Identify the additional training, qualifications and experience you need to gain. Define the critical elements in each of these areas. Each of these tasks then becomes an individual target that can be subdivided into further detailed steps. Your training could be broken down to areas such as prospecting, building rapport, identifying customer needs, presentation skills, overcoming objections, closing the sale, and customer service.

Each of the individual areas of training can be further subdivided into immediate or short term goals. Prioritise and sequence what needs to be done. Set a time-line. All of your focus and action can then be targeted to achieving your goals. Your immediate priority of achieving your short term goals moves you towards your medium term goals. All the time you keep your longer term goals in mind.

Once you have established your medium and short term goals, you can prioritise your daily tasks. You will understand which tasks contribute directly to your goals. You will also know which tasks do not contribute to your goals. You can then choose to ignore or delegate these tasks as appropriate.

The advantage of setting goals

Setting goals will help you to:

- Know where you are going.
- Have a frame of reference.
- Stay on track.
- Uncover your potential.
- Reach your targets.
- Maintain stability.
- Stay motivated.
- Remain accountable.
- Make the right decisions.
- Take control of your workload.
- Improve your self-confidence.
- Focus on your priorities.
- Eliminate bad habits.
- Optimise available resources.
- Reduce any stress or anxiety.
- Achieve job satisfaction.

Why most people fail to set goals

Most people fail to set personal goals. The main reasons are that:

- They do not recognise the benefits of setting goals.
- They do not believe in the benefits of goal setting.
- They do not know how to set goals.
- They have had previous negative experiences with poor goal setting.
- They lack self-belief.
- They fear failure.
- They are stuck in their comfort zone.

- They are satisfied with what they have already achieved.
- They want it now. Their focus is on the here and now.

What happens without goals?

Without goals any road will get you there. Without goals you will be leaving outcome to chance. Without goals you will lack vision and purpose. Without goals you will be destined for mediocrity.

People who do not set goals tend to be unhappy and unsuccessful in life. Their actions are dictated by others. They work to other peoples' priorities. They are followers, rather than leaders. They react to events, rather than being proactive. They get caught up in their day to day activities. They are busy without being productive. They do not make plans for the future. Without goals they wander aimlessly through life.

Without goals people will focus on what they do not want. They will concentrate on problems and concerns. They will become anxious and restless.

The benefits of your goals

Consider the reasons why you want to achieve your goals. Think about the benefits that will accrue. Having at least one major reason for achieving your goals helps to provide the impetus you need. So your goal may be to become sales director, but the reason may be to have a better house and company car.

Common reasons for setting long term goals might be:

- To improve your earnings.
- To enhance your savings.
- Status and recognition.
- A bigger house.
- A new car.
- Job satisfaction.
- To progress in your career.
- Additional power and influence.
- Early retirement.
- Setting up your own business.
- Purchasing a holiday home.

If you have a clear, definite reason for your goals you will be motivated to continue to work towards them. It helps you stay committed to achieving your goals. The benefits accrued from achieving your goals must outweigh the cost of the effort involved. This is essential in order to overcome the inevitable obstacles you will encounter along the way. It is one of the core motivational drivers to achieving the success that you desire.

Set your own goals for yourself

You must set your own long term goals for yourself. A goal that you define and set for yourself will instil more motivation than any goals that are set by someone else. The critical factor is that you must believe in your goals. If you are to lead others and convince them to follow you, then you must have passion and commitment.

Your goals should reflect your own personal values and beliefs. Think about what is important to you. Think about how you want to develop as a person.

What type of leader do you want to become? How would you like others to describe you? How would you want your epitaph to describe your life? Your personal goals should reinforce your core moral standards. They should uplift you. Concentrate on your essential values. Remain true to yourself.

Set realistic short term goals

There should be no limit to the level of your long term goals. It is better to aim high and miss than to aim low and hit. The important thing is that you commit to your goals.

However your short term goals should be realistic and achievable. You should take into account the available resources. You should set a realistic time frame.

Set SMART goals

Goals should be SMART:

- Specific, clearly defined, precise and understandable.
- Measurable, having quantifiable results.
- Attainable, realistic and feasible.
- Relevant and meaningful to what you want to achieve.
- Time-bound, having a target date for completion.

Guidelines for setting goals

- State your goal in a positive way.
- Quantify your goals.
- Specifying target dates.
- Write down your goals.
- Break larger goals down into smaller more

achievable targets.
- Prioritise your goals.
- Set goals that you can control.
- Set realistic goals.

Set progressively more difficult goals

If you are tackling something new it is advisable to set
progressively more difficult goals. The nature of
learning is that we begin by mastering the simple
tasks. This motivates us to try something more
challenging. We then tackle more difficult tasks as we
gain in confidence and self-belief. Eventually we gain
enough experience to carry out the most arduous tasks.
We set our sights on bigger targets. We can take
anything in our stride. We achieve more than we ever
thought possible at the outset.

Allow a degree of flexibility

Allow a degree of flexibility in your goals. Your long
term goals are likely to change with time. As you
grow and develop your needs and expectations will
change. You will not be the same person at forty that
you were at twenty. Your journey does not need to be
in a straight line.

Setting priorities

You should focus on activities that move you towards
your goals. You should minimise activities that do not
contribute towards your goals.

Taking action

Winning starts with beginning. Once your priorities

have been set and a plan has been devised it is time to set the wheels in motion. You cannot win by playing safe. You must take the necessary action in order to get the desired outcome. You must take calculated risks if you want to achieve anything of lasting value.

There is always a cost involved in reaching your goals. There will be the inevitable sacrifices you have to make along the way. There will be difficulties and obstacles along the journey. You will sometimes have to overcome self-doubts and fear. You will be criticised by others, even close friends. There will be times when you must neglect the things and people that are important to you in order to retain your focus on the desired outcome. You will have to pay the cost that comes along with success. You must always keep the long term benefits in mind. Remain focused on the outcome as you take the necessary steps towards your destination.

Reaching milestones

Setting milestones enables you to stay motivated. Celebrate reaching each milestone along the way.

Personal mission statement

Consider making a personal mission statement. Your mission statement should focus on your career and personal aspirations. It should reflect your values and beliefs.

You can display your mission statement in your home study as a source of inspiration.

Chapter 8. Planning

Plan in advance

Allow yourself time to plan things properly. Planning is a process of thinking things through. It is a process of deciding on a course of action to achieve your goals. Planning is an essential stage if you want to make the best use of your time and to succeed in your endeavours. Planning is required to ensure that you take the right approach. Planning is needed in order to prioritise work, reserve the required resources and allocate the tasks to your team members. You must schedule time for planning at the beginning and end of every day.

You should always carry a small notebook and pen to jot down ideas during the day as you interact with others. You can incorporate these ideas in your plans. Do not rely on memory alone.

Advantages of planning

Planning allows you to:

- Set objectives.
- Prioritise activities.
- Budget costs.
- Ensure availability of resources.
- Allocate resources economically.
- Ensure that deadlines are met.
- Ensure that goals are achieved.
- Avoid emergency and unforeseen events
- Communicate purpose.

Practise and rehearse

If you are going to give a presentation, make a proposal, attend an interview or take part in an important performance then you should rehearse in advance. Visualise your performance. Imagine how you will succeed in making your points. Rehearsing helps you to work out better ways of presenting your case. The more you rehearse the better you will get. Proper preparation enhances self-confidence. It improves your confidence and helps you to make a favourable impression.

Chapter 9. Setting goals for your team

Set clear goals

As a leader you must define your team's purpose and direction. You must know what you expect your team to achieve. You must communicate this to each member of your team. Each team member must understand his individual role and how he is to interact with the rest of the team.

You must gain the commitment of every member of your team. You must inspire them by your energy and enthusiasm. You must stress the importance of their work. You must communicate with your team and listen to their suggestions. Their actions are your actions. You are accountable. You will be judged by their success or failure.

The company mission statement

Look at the company mission statement. Think about how it relates to your department. Draw up a similar statement to cover the main goals of your department. Better still give this as an exercise for your team to complete. This will help your team to focus on what is important. It will help in the setting of priorities.

Set consistent goals

Be consistent in your goal setting. Avoid competing priorities. This only adds to confusion on which task needs to be completed first. Avoid shifting priorities where you tell someone to do one thing one day and the opposite thing the next day. Stay focused on your goals and the results needed to get you there.

Set targets that can be achieved

You must set individual targets that can be achieved. These targets should ideally be expressed in terms of a quantifiable figure. An example would be to sell 100 products per month. The targets should be agreed with the individual concerned in advance. They should be related to the key responsibilities of the job. The targets must match the competence of the individual concerned. It is acceptable to include a degree of stretch so that the individual is challenged by the task. However they must know where and how they can access assistance. Allow sufficient time and resources to help them achieve the task.

Specify standards

You must specify the standards required in carrying out the job. You can do this by keeping written specifications or by communicating them directly when you delegate work. The standards ensure that the work is carried out to the correct quality requirements.

Results oriented

Your team needs to be results, not task, orientated. If your team knows the required results they can alter the plan for themselves if things begin to go wrong. If people are focused on the task they can end up diverted from the required destination.

Measure performance

Once you have set the goals for each member of your team you must devise a means of measuring performance to ensure that goals are being met on target and to specification.

Review performance

You must review performance regularly. This does not need to be in a formal environment. While there is a need for annual reviews your job should involve giving daily feedback on performance. Every piece of work that is returned to you deserves to have some form of feed back. This may be a simple thank you, open praise for a job well done or private constructive feedback on how to improve performance next time.

Chapter 10. Communicating

Improving communication skills

Effective communication is an essential skill in the business environment. Employers value leaders who can communicate effectively by oral and written means. Successful communication promotes understanding, builds rapport, improves relationships and avoids misunderstanding and disagreement. Communication is essential in motivating team members and building morale. You must work continuously on improving your communication skills if you want to be an effective leader.

Unfortunately our education systems concentrate on teaching us to read and write while ignoring the need to listen and talk. In business it is the ability to listen that is most important, followed by the ability to talk. Writing and reading are much less important. Written memos are often ignored, over looked and forgotten. People pay much more attention to what is said, particularly if the message is simple and reinforced by repetition.

Be aware of your own body language

You must first of all be aware of your own body language when you are communicating. You must be able to control your body language in order to achieve the desired outcome. If your body language is backing up the verbal message then you will be believed. This will enable you to influence others more easily.

If your body language is in conflict with what you are

trying to say then it will undermine what you are saying. You will be sending mixed signals. The listener will pay more attention to your body language. They will not believe what you are saying. You will have difficulty convincing them to do what you want.

Face-to-face communication

Where possible use face-to-face communication. People look for the visual impact of body language. Over half of the message is conveyed in this manner. Observing body language allows you to get immediate feedback. You can gauge the success or otherwise of your communication from the body language of the other person. The visual message is very important in communication. If you need to explain something that is technical, complicated or sensitive then make sure you meet the person face-to-face. Remember that receiving messages is just as important as transmitting them.

Vocal message

How you say something is more important than what you say. You must learn to use the correct tone of voice. Introducing inflection and changes in tone, pace and volume of speech can all improve the way that the message is received.

Have an objective

Focus on the outcome you want. Do you want to create awareness, impart knowledge, project an image, influence a decision, alter behaviour, stimulate a want or desire, or close a sale? Keep the end result in mind and focus on how you can achieve this.

Keep it short and simple

Keep your message short and simple. Do not over complicate your instructions. Keep to one point at a time. Do not confuse people. Be aware that words mean different things to different people. Use simple plain language and short sentences. Only ask one question at a time.

How to improve your communication

In order to communicate effectively with others at work you must:

- Prepare what you will say in advance.
- Use the correct communication medium for the occasion.
- Select the right audience or recipient.
- Avoid sending the message through several layers of the organisation. It may become distorted.
- Communicate face-to-face rather than by e-mail or written word.
- Choose the correct venue.
- Choose the correct time, when the recipient is willing and able to receive the message.
- Ask for feedback.
- Keep the message short and simple.
- Keep to the point.
- Re-emphasise the main points to reinforce the message.
- Use simple plain language.
- Use more than one channel of communication. A presentation could use visual, oral and written media to get the message across.
- Speak clearly and audibly.
- Use precise language that the listener can understand.
- Avoid jargon.

- Listen actively.
- Look at body language.
- Give feedback.
- Do not interrupt.

Withholding information

Be aware of the dangers of withholding information. If you issue different information to different groups on a need to know basis you will set up barriers. People who are left out of the chain will feel aggrieved and undervalued. If the information pertains to an individual or a group then you should make it available to them unless there is a very specific reason for not doing so.

The importance of listening

All great leaders know and recognise the importance of listening. With a one-to-one conversation you should listen at least twice as much as you talk. In a group discussion you should consume no more than 20% of the time talking. Your input should only be to set the topic, keep people on track, encourage suggestions, summarise agreement and confirm any decisions. Listening enables you to:

- Acquire information.
- Gauge acceptance.
- Clarify issues.
- Make better decisions.
- Diagnose problems.
- Resolve conflict.
- Show respect.
- Display empathy.
- Build understanding.
- Build rapport.

- Build trust.
- Improve motivation.

Unfortunately most people do not appreciate the importance of listening properly. Most conversations are just intersecting monologues.

It is vital that you learn to listen effectively. People appreciate it when you listen, particularly if they are feeling vulnerable. People know when you are not listening properly. If you do not listen properly it sends a very clear signal that you do not care. When listening to someone, do not spend your time thinking about what you want to say next. You may miss some important point. You will not be able to build trust and influence people if you do not listen properly.

Barriers to listening

Listening is the most important element of communication. Most people do not listen effectively. They do not receive the signals being sent to them. There can be a number of reasons for this:

- They are not concentrating.
- They are bored.
- They are too preoccupied with their own thoughts.
- They are thinking about what they are going to say next.
- They are unable to understand the message.
- They are uninterested in the message.

Barriers to receiving the message

The human senses can receive up to 11 million bits of information per second. We can only process 40 bits of information per second and we can only store 7 bits of information at the one time in our conscious mind. Therefore we ignore most of the data that we are capable of picking up. Our eyes will concentrate on what is moving and ignore static objects. Our ears will filter out repetitive background noise, such as a ticking clock, and concentrate on loud or unusual noises than might signal danger. Much of the information that we receive from our senses is deleted, distorted or generalised before we process it. This enables us to function by concentrating on what we perceive to be of importance.

Sometimes we cannot, or do not want to, receive the message. There is effectively a barrier between the sender of the message and the listener or receiver. The barrier may be caused by:

- Different interpretation of words or meaning.
- Hearing what we want to hear.
- Ignoring anything that conflicts with our beliefs or prejudices.
- Dislike for the person who is speaking.
- Ignoring messages from rival groups.
- Message sent through the wrong medium.
- Conflict between the speaker's words and body language.
- Overload – too much irrelevant information.
- Background noise.
- Distractions.
- The receiver being emotionally or physically incapable of receiving the message.

Proactive listening

Listening tends to be regarded as a passive skill when in fact the secret to successful listening is to actively participate with the speaker. Listening skills can be improved by the following actions:

- Maintaining eye contact.
- Concentrating on the speaker, including his body language.
- Nodding and making sounds of encouragement.
- Asking questions.
- Summarising and reflecting back what the speaker has said.
- Mentally evaluating the message.

Proactive listening enables you to receive, interpret and understand the message. It enables you to appreciate the speaker's viewpoint and feelings. By improving your listening skills you can build rapport with the speaker. The speaker will feel that you are genuinely interested in them and what they have to say. Proactive listening is vital in business when dealing with your team, superiors, clients, customers or suppliers.

Mistakes to avoid when listening

There are a number of mistakes you must avoid when listening to someone else:

- Interrupting the speaker.
- Changing the topic.
- Talking about your concerns.
- Well intentioned comments.
- Criticising, advising, diagnosing, baiting.
- Concentrating on what you will say next.
- Pretending that you understand.
- Talking too much.
- Correcting the speaker.

Ask questions

People will commence a conversation for a specific reason. However they do not always get to the point. Sometimes they want to broach something with their boss, but are not sure of the reaction they will get. So they talk about something else in order to get a chance to see what kind of mood their boss is in.

Listen carefully to what your employees say. Establish eye contact. Ask questions to elicit more information. Get them to open up. Ask them how they feel about things. Do not criticise, argue or patronise your employees. Probe for further information, but be careful that the conversation does not turn into an interrogation. You can avoid this by relating to your own circumstances and showing empathy. Eventually you will get to the stage where they are willing to share their concerns. At this stage you can ask questions that would not have got a response at the outset of the conversation.

Create Empathy

Empathy involves sensing and understanding someone else's feelings and concerns. It involves understanding the other person's perspective without judgement. It involves demonstrating that you are sensitive to their feelings. It involves tuning into the other person's wavelength and creating resonance. It involves echoing their ideas and feelings. It involves speaking the same language. Empathy involves connecting with the other person's thoughts and emotions. It involves reaching accord and agreement.

While still remaining objective and detached you can convey that you appreciate the other person's feelings and emotions. Empathy occurs when:

- You respect the views of the other person.
- You respect the needs and concerns of the other person.
- You actively listen.
- You display interest in what is being said.
- You value their feelings and attitudes.
- You reassure people that you care.
- You accept people for what they are.
- You are open and responsive in your body language and communication..
- You create an environment where others can express their feelings.
- You refrain from judgement and apportioning blame.
- You refrain from offering unwanted advice.
- You help others to find a solution.

By displaying empathy you can build trust and get other people to respond positively. The more you care about people the stronger the relationships you will build. Conversely if someone feels that you do not care about them you will not be able to build a constructive working relationship with that person.

Build rapport

Displaying empathy with others is a great way of building rapport. Showing a genuine interest in others will help build rapport. Listening actively to others, talking about their interests and asking about their progress all help to build rapport.

Pay attention to body language

Pay attention to someone's body language when they are talking to you. Does their body language back up what they are saying? If not, they may have some concern that they are reluctant to voice. Listen for signs of hesitancy or doubt. What is the underlying message? Think about why they may have broached a topic. Ask them if there are any concerns. Encourage them to open up.

Look out for signs that people want to speak in group discussions. They may have a valid point that needs to be aired and discussed. Look for signs of confusion. You may need to clarify a point. You must become as adept at listening for what is not said as well as the actual words that are spoken.

Listen for objections

A large part of your job as a leader is to delegate work and to try to influence others. It is important when communicating with others that you also listen carefully to the response. Pay attention to body language and what is not being said. There may be a reluctance to comply or an objection to your proposals. Subordinates are very wary of voicing objections. They may have spotted some problem with your proposal. Remember that they are closer to the work than you are. They will understand all the implications better than you do. If there is a legitimate reason for altering your proposal it is better to detect it up front before the company spends time and resources on it.

Distinguish between facts and opinions

When someone is talking to you they will convey a mixture of facts and opinions. Make sure that you distinguish between the two. You must understand the difference between objective information and subjective beliefs. You may want to take action based on the facts.

However you need to be wary of any proposed action based on opinions.

Do not interrupt

Do not interrupt people when they are talking. It shows a lack of respect. Often people pause to collect their thoughts, before continuing with their conversation. Make sure that someone has finished their point before you respond.

Do not change the topic

Do not change the topic when people are talking. It is disrespectful. It implies that your interests are more important than those of the speaker. Changing the topic implies that you do not care about a person's views or about them as an individual.

Summarise

When winding the conversation up you should summarise what has been agreed, the action that needs to be taken and the time line. You may have misinterpreted something. By summarising you will be able to confirm that you have received the message correctly.

Listening on the phone

If you are listening to someone on the phone you do not have the benefit of observing their body language. It is therefore even more important to listen carefully to the message. On mobile phones you have the added problem of poor signals. Yet how many people do we see talking on the phone and doing other things at the same time, like reading memos or searching through drawers or files. Give the other person your undivided attention. Multitasking does not work. You may miss an essential element of the conversation. You will have to ask the other person to repeat himself. It will be obvious to the other person that you are not listening properly. This is sending a signal that you do not care about them. You do not respect them enough to pay your full attention to what they are trying to tell you.

Chapter 11. Team building

Definition of team

A team is a small group of people brought together for a common purpose. The ideal team will have skills that are complimentary. They will work collaboratively to achieve common objectives.

The requirements of a successful team

There are four key requirements for a team to function effectively:

- Trust in one another.
- Open, frank discussion on objectives and methods.
- Putting team goals before individual objectives.
- Holding each other to account if the effort is lacking.

Trust

As well as trusting their leader a team must have a deep trust in one another. Trust is a shared belief that the team members can depend on one another to achieve their common goals. Trust is the basic building block for relationships. Trust develops through openness, honesty, empathy, fair treatment, a shared bond, integrity, delivering on promises and consistency.

Team members must be open and honest with one another. They must be frank about their weaknesses, fears and concerns as well as celebrating their strengths. Team members should be able to openly admit mistakes to one another without fear that this knowledge will be utilised against them.

As a leader you must help to build this trust between the members of your team. You must hold regular briefing meetings with your team and encourage them to trust and believe in one another.

In a soccer game a defender is only confident and free to attack when he has the knowledge that other players will cover his position until he returns after the attacking move has ended. Temporarily he will adapt an attacking role. He cannot carry out both defending and attacking roles at the same time. His concentration is 100% focused on what he is doing. He cannot look back to see if anyone has covered for him in defence. He must trust his team mates to do what is right for the team.

In the military the very lives of each team member is reliant on the professionalism of the other team members. There has to be total trust. In a fire fight if you are heavily outnumbered then you must enter the zone and concentrate on what you are doing. You must trust that the other team members are doing the right thing. If their job is to lay down covering fire while you are moving to a better position, then you must trust them to do so. If a member of the team gets injured he trusts the medics to provide first aid. He trusts his comrades to extract him from the danger zone. He also trusts his commander to call in an aircraft to get him to the field hospital as soon as possible.

Work teams cannot function to their potential unless there is total and unconditional trust in one another.

Frank debate

You should hold regular weekly meetings with your team. Encourage each team member to give their honest opinion on anything that they disagree with. Ask for suggestions on anything that they think could be done better. The aim is to improve the overall effectiveness of the team. Any activity that the team carries out should be open for debate. By getting issues out in the open you can deal with them to the satisfaction of the team.

There will not be unanimous agreement on all issues. However the minority will have had a proper chance to air their views and listen to the reasoning and opinion of others. This is much better than harbouring resentment or mistrust. Problems or issues that are not resolved always fester and lead to greater relationship difficulties. This will hamper the effectiveness of any team. It is much better to have open and frank debate. Once a decision has been made all team members must give it 100% backing.

All debate must concentrate on the issues at hand. There should not be any personal recriminations.
Team members must respect the views of others even if they do not agree with them. Disagreement can be healthy when both parties have the interests of the team foremost in their minds.

Frank and open debate which takes into account the views of each member of the team almost always leads to better decision making. It certainly leads to better acceptance of the collective decisions.

Putting the team first

Every member of the team must put the objectives of the team before any individual desires. The team must come first and foremost. Everything else is secondary. The fact that an individual team member may have a different view on how things should be done is irrelevant. He must get on with his duties and support his team in their objective.

As a leader you must measure the team's success on the achievements of its goals. Individual performance is a secondary issue. The fact that two players had an outstanding game is of no consequence if the team gets beaten.

Each member of the team must focus on attaining team results. Team members must be willing to help one another in the overall interests of the team. If the team fails, everyone fails. Individual mistakes happen, but team members are there to cover for one another. If the overall objective was not met, then everyone must accept responsibility. Everyone must review their own performance. The team must review practices and procedures. They must alter the plan next time if that is what is required.

If members set aside individual career aspirations, departmental interests and other personal concerns, then they will achieve more by supporting the team than they would be working in isolation. If the team is successful then longer term rewards will come and all team members will benefit.

Holding one another to account

Everyone has a role to play. Everyone must understand their own role and that of the other team members. In a sport such as soccer everyone has a nominal position on the pitch and will play in that role for the majority of the time. However they will interact with team mates and support one another. They will alter their position depending on which team has the ball, where the attack is developing and the position taken up by team mates and the opposition.

As the game proceeds the position is fluid and rapidly changing. Mistakes are made and possession is given away. Players get tired and concentration lapses. Players get injured and are temporarily out of the game. There is a need to cover and a need to communicate rapidly. There will be shouts of encouragement from some players and frank and terse criticism from others. Fingers will be pointed as one player is told by another to get into position and cover an attacking player. There will be open criticism as well as support and encouragement. Exchanges will be brief but honest.

The same feedback is required in all teams if they are to be a success. The team can plan and practise for any task and will often take into account different circumstances. However this is no substitution for the actual circumstances that can unfold at times. Unforeseen events do happen. A crisis or emergency can occur. This will involve members having to support one another and possibly criticising one another.

Holding one another to account is essential if the team is to reach its objective. It is usually too late to wait until the event is over. More often than not the leader will not be present when a difficulty arises. It is up to the team to make the right decisions and to alter course if required. If someone is not putting in the required effort then others must point it out. It is better if a team can resolve its problems without having to involve the leader. Team members can use a mixture of constructive criticism and encouragement to get the desired behaviour from one another. In an atmosphere of trust team members will be willing to accept advise of this nature from one another.

Create a shared vision

A shared vision provides team members with a clear sense of direction. People often find their own ways of getting somewhere once they know the destination.

Clarify roles

Make sure that everyone knows exactly what their role is and what is expected of them. They should also know the role of others and how they are expected to interact with one another. They should know what is expected of them when things are going well. They should also know what to do in adverse conditions when pressure is concentrated on themselves or someone else.

Get commitment

Get commitment from each member of your team. Everyone must buy in to each objective. They are all entitled to air their views and they will not all agree on the methods involved for any given task. However, they must all be committed once a decision has been made on the best way to proceed.

Make targets progressively more challenging

Set progressively more challenging targets. Initial targets should be easy to achieve. By reaching these targets confidence will be built at an early stage. Team members will be motivated to continue.

Provide the best resources

Provide the best resources you can get for your team. Provide the best office facilities and computer equipment you can afford. Any tools or equipment should be the best that you can afford. Training should be ongoing, targeted and effective. If you want to get the best results then make sure that resources are not an issue.

Provide focus

A leader's main task is to keep the group focused on their objectives. Remove distractions and sources of conflict from the working environment. Keep the team focused on the desired outcome.

Maintain a comfortable working environment

Avoid introducing tension or stress into the working environment. As the leader of your group it is up to you to set the tone. If you behave in a stressed manner the rest of the group will pick up on this and this will lead to a tense working environment.

Trust your team

Trust your team to reach their targets. After you have delegated work, allow them to get on with it. Do not micromanage people. You must be open and honest with your team. You must encourage them to come forward with any issues that they have. You must give them the responsibility to make their own decisions.

Hold regular team meetings

Hold regular review meetings. Get feedback and suggestions from team members. Encourage openness and frankness.

Give effective feedback

You must give regular effective feedback to each team member. When they have completed an assignment for you, take time to review it with them. Ask them for their views on the work. Find out if there were any areas where they experienced difficulty. Offer advice where you can. Praise any aspects of the work that were carried out well. Do all of this first.

Only when you have praised the work and asked for their opinion should you move onto talking about areas that might be improved. You must be very tactful on how you do this. Do not talk about the person. Talk about the work and the objectives. Make it clear that the objective of the feedback is to help the other person attain their personal goals.

Do not say, "You could have done this better". This automatically provokes a defensive, emotional reaction. You have attacked their sense of worth. You are questioning their effort and their ability.
It is much better to say, "I wondered if this part could have been presented in the following way. What do you think of that suggestion?" This way you are concentrating on the work and not the personality. You are offering an opinion and not a judgement. You are also encouraging them to think about your feedback and to respond with their thoughts.

Constructive feedback will always reap more benefit that open criticism. It removes emotional distractions, it encourages self assessment and it helps to build trust. If your team members respect you as a leader they will also respect your opinions and your experience. They will listen to any advice you give. They will appreciate the tactful manner in which it is offered.

Be professional in your dealings with your team. Remain calm and objective. Encourage your team to perform to their potential. This approach helps to build trust and support.

Work to the strengths of your team

Different team members have different strengths and skills. As a leader you should recognise this when assigning tasks. Get people to specialise in what they do best. This is the best way to get the optimum overall performance from your team.

Involve everyone

Involve all team members in what you are trying to achieve. Do not leave anyone out, regardless of their ability or level of enthusiasm. Everyone must feel that they have a valid input to make. Their views must be recognised and accepted.

Step back

Learn to step back so that others can step forward. Do not dominate discussions and meetings. Maintain control but let others give their input.

Chapter 12. Motivating your team

The ability to motivate others is key to the success or otherwise of a leader. Motivating people involves getting them to move in the direction that you want them to.

If you ask leaders to rate their motivational skills they will score themselves highly. If you ask team members to rate their leaders on motivational skills you will get a much lower score. The problem is that many leaders pay lip service to the importance of motivation. They do not take the time and effort to apply motivational techniques when dealing with their subordinates.

Carrot or stick

There are two opposite ways to motivate someone to do something. You can either reward them for achieving results or punish them for failing to do so. Rewarding people is much more productive and will get the results you want. This chapter will focus on the many ways in which you can offer short and long term rewards. As a leader you will get what you reward.

Punishment or the threat of punishment should be avoided whenever possible. Punishment is a tool of last resort. Punishment focuses on the negative. It creates a poor working environment. It lacks incentive to improve performance. It encourages fear, resentment and insecurity.

Basic social needs

Motivational theory is based on the fact that people have

basic social needs that must be satisfied. You must administer to these needs in every member of your team and in others that you deal with in the workplace. These social needs include a sense of recognition, acceptance, appreciation, encouragement, assistance, fellowship and equal treatment. When you look at these needs it is immediately evident that you can meet almost all of them through effective communication. By listening to concerns and interests and caring about people you will build trust and loyalty.

If you provide these basic needs you will help your team members to feel a sense of achievement, responsibility and personal growth. Most people leave their bosses and not their jobs. The main reason that they leave is because they do not feel valued.

Recognise achievements

Recognition is a powerful motivator. People want to know that they have done a good job and that you appreciate their efforts. They do not want to be taken for granted. Recognise and acknowledge the individual achievements of every single member of your team. Do this every day if you can.

Celebrate success by rewarding your team. Reward minor successes with small rewards. Reward major successes with more substantial rewards. Remember people's birthdays with a card and a cake.

Longer term recognition involves financial rewards in terms of pay rises or bonuses as well as promotion.

Accept people for what they are

As a leader you will strive to get the best from each individual. However you must also accept each individual for what he is. Do not be judgemental. You must recognise and take advantage of the diversity in people. Differences in talents and abilities do not make people better or worse than anyone else. A successful team needs many strengths and people to carry out different functions.

People learn at different rates and in different ways. Focus on their good points and let them work to their strengths. Do not focus on and punish their weaknesses. Instead provide the resources where they can get the proper training to increase their skill base. Provide encouragement and support. Accept the unique skills and attributes that each person brings to your team. Make people feel that they are a valued member of your team. Treat them with the respect they deserve.

Offer praise

Recognise and praise work of a high standard. Offer praise in public. Praise a person face to face. Praise should be given when the desired behaviour is exhibited, not later. Show appreciation for effort as well as results. Be specific about what you are praising. Give credit to your team whenever you can. Do not accept credit for their efforts. Let it be known what they have contributed.

Praise costs you nothing. However most managers only offer praise on rare occasions. This is one of the fundamental errors in management behaviour. You should praise your team every day. A simple "Thank you, well done, that was excellent work," takes less than five seconds to say, but it makes the world of difference to the person receiving the praise. Praise motivates your team and builds loyalty and trust. Try not to follow praise with criticism. Leave constructive criticism to another time.

Encourage your team

You must encourage the members of your team if they are facing adversity. Encouragement should also be provided when they make mistakes. Words of encouragement provide the confidence to continue when the seeds of doubt are beginning to creep into people's minds. Encourage people by restating your confidence in their skills and their abilities.

Encourage people before they begin a task. If you tell someone that you know that they will do a great job, then this is exactly what will transpire. People will not want to let you down. Praise and encouragement cost you nothing, yet they yield amazing results.

Encourage members to assist one another

Provide a climate in which help is available when required. Encourage team members to help one another. Team members should have skills and knowledge that compliment one another. Encourage them to assist one another to help with workloads or when specialist knowledge is required. Mutual support can create a sense of camaraderie.

Foster a sense of belonging

Foster a sense of belonging for every member of your team. No one should feel excluded from the team. You need to build a sense of camaraderie where the input of everyone is welcomed and appreciated.

Treat everyone the same

As a leader you must treat every member of your team in the same manner. You should treat them as you would like to be treated yourself. They are going to make mistakes. Allow them to do so. It is an essential element of the learning process. You are there for them to turn to for advice and help when they need it. You are also there to coach them and steer them in the right direction. You are not there to harangue, bully or intimidate them. This will be counter-productive and will lead to failure for the team and ultimately failure for you as a leader.

Provide adequate material needs

At times people will request that you provide certain material needs to help them with their jobs. They may also ask about certain training opportunities. They will sometimes ask you to intervene on their behalf with others to represent their interests. It is important that you make any such requests a priority. Make sure that you honour any commitments to resolve such issues.

Resolve conflict promptly

Resolve conflict promptly before it has a chance to escalate. Conflict damages moral and is counter-productive. Stamp it out at the first sign. Investigate and resolve any issues in a fair manner. Do not let team members become distracted from their goals by the negative consequences of unresolved conflict.

Goals

To motivate people you must first provide goals. Setting goals helps people to achieve their basic needs.

Individuals should participate in the setting of their own goals. Goals should be specific, challenging and achievable. Positive and constructive feedback should be provided as people work towards their goals. Continual reinforcement can be provided by offering incentives or rewards for effort and achievement as individual milestones are reached.

Expectancy theory

In order to change behaviour an individual must value the reward for the effort more than the cost involved. There must be a clear link between the reward and the effort. In order to persevere, a person must appreciate the benefits of achieving the desired outcome.

Intrinsic motivation

Intrinsic motivation consists of the internal factors that cause a person to want to complete tasks because of the inherent satisfaction involved. Intrinsic motivational factors include satisfaction in a job well done and a sense of achievement. People are motivated by the opportunity to make a difference and the chance to improve their skills. They like to solve challenging problems. They prefer responsibility and the opportunity for personal growth. Intrinsic motivators tend to last longer as they can be deeply ingrained in an individual.

Extrinsic motivation

Extrinsic factors such as money or rewards can be used to motivate employees. Extrinsic factors can also be negative. Examples include punishment or criticism for inappropriate behaviour or lack of effort.

There are no simple answers

Motivation is a complex and sometimes unpredictable process. There are no simple formulae to improve motivation. Individual needs and aspirations vary. The degree of intrinsic and extrinsic motivational factors is difficult to balance for each individual. The expectation of rewards also differs greatly amongst different employees.

Ask them what they want

Each individual is motivated by something different. Therefore the simplest way to work out what motivates each member of your team is to ask them. Meet with them individually and ask them about what they value most in a job. What is it they would like to be provided with to help them perform better? Find out if it is praise, recognition, autonomy, achieving more, encouragement, money, bonuses or promotion that motivates them. Once you know you can then press the correct buttons for each member of your team.

Inspire them

You must inspire people if you are to motivate them. People will feed off your enthusiasm.

Be available

Make sure that you are available to answer queries. Make time every day to be available for your staff. Let them know in advance when you are available. People appreciate it when you give them your time. Conversely it is bad for morale if work is delayed while people are waiting for your input.

Listen and empathise

Listen to what your team members tell you. Listen to their ideas. Forget about yourself and pay attention to their concerns. Empathise with them. Demonstrate your respect for them. Support them whenever possible. Show that you care.

Give them a choice

Let people volunteer for assignments of their choice whenever possible. People will pick projects in which they are interested and from which they hope to gain the right experience and contacts. Regardless of their motives, if they have volunteered they will be more committed to achieving the results you want.

Show the whole picture

If you explain the importance of a task it helps to motivate people to complete the task. Show how the task fits into the overall strategy. Also by communicating how the company is performing on a monthly basis you will keep people interested in how their work is contributing to overall goals. If your department is carrying out one particular aspect of the companies goals try and get this metric included in monthly company reports. People will be motivated to improve if they can see the figure published in this way.

Provide a sense of purpose

People prefer to work on things that matter to them. Try to allocate the work by taking into consideration the interests and aspirations of each individual. They must be able to feel a sense of achievement.

Expect the best from people

Let people know that you expect the best from them and that you are confident in their ability to deliver. Then leave them free to do just that. If you show faith in their ability they will come to believe in themselves also. Do not micromanage. Encourage your team to show initiative and come up with solutions.

Lead by example

Set an example for others to follow. Motivation begins with a good example. What you do says more about you as a leader than what you say. Know the way, go the way and show the way. While you may judge yourself by what you are capable of doing others will judge you by your actions. Do not force others to take the right path. Lead the way and let them follow your example. Lead, do not drive.

Build morale

Build morale through effective communication.

Build trust

Trust takes time to build up, but can be quickly destroyed. You must build mutual trust, mutual care, mutual respect and mutual support between yourself and every member of your team.

Be loyal

Be loyal to the members of your team. Represent their interests. Defend them when necessary.

Avoid criticising

Try to avoid giving out criticism where possible. Never, ever criticise someone in front of someone else. Never refer to the quality of a team member's work when speaking to their peers. Never criticise, abuse or embarrass members of your team. Once you have lost the trust, confidence or respect of an employee, you may never get it back.

Provide flexible arrangements

Provide flexible working arrangements for your staff. They will appreciate it if you take into account their family commitments. You just need to ensure that they are available for team meetings and any collective briefings or project work. You should not wish to restrict them further.

Provide individual autonomy

Provide adequate training so that people can master the required skills to perform well in their jobs. This will add to their sense of achievement. If they have performed consistently well then give them a degree of autonomy to set goals and devise their own methods of achieving them. Let them look after their own budgets, allocate resources, make decisions and set priorities. Autonomy is a longer term reward for consistent high performance.

Empower your team

People like to be in charge of their own work. Let your team exercise control over and take responsibility for their work. Let them develop their own ideas and make their own decisions. Do not be the decision making bottleneck holding up progress. Provide them with the right guidelines and resources and then let them get on with it. They know their jobs better than anyone else. They are in the perfect position to make decisions about the best way to carry out the work. Empowerment gives people more control over their own destiny. It speeds up decision making. It cuts out bureaucracy. It reduces operational costs.

In the absence of empowerment you have a situation of command and control. The problem with this system is that people will carry out an individual command then wait until you become available to issue the next command. The process is task oriented. Team members do not think for themselves. They are not permitted to show initiative.

Bonuses or rewards

The problem with bonus or rewards is that money is not the thing that motivates people most. So if you introduce some kind of bonus do not expect dramatic results. The second problem with bonuses is that, after a period of time, people come to expect them as a right rather than a reward. Bonuses are only effective in the short term. It is useful therefore to change the method in which a bonus is structured and calculated every year. Just let people know in advance that the scheme will only run for a year.

To be effective bonuses or rewards must be:

- Linked to organisational goals.
- Reinforce desired behaviour.
- Discourage undesired behaviour.
- Focused on desired performance levels.

Promotion

In the longer term you need to promote the high achievers. This is the only way to retain good staff. If you want to keep high performing employees then you must recognise that the skills and experience that they have developed have made them more valuable to the company. If you do not pay the going rate, someone else will be only too happy to do so. If you lose good people you then need to repeat the expensive process of recruiting and training replacements.

Chapter 13. Developing your team

People are your most important asset

People are the most important asset of a company. Unfortunately many companies and managers do not treat them as they should. Just like any asset or working capital, there is a cost involved in acquiring and maintaining people. In order to get a decent return on their investment companies should nourish and develop their people. If they do not, then their productivity will wither and die on the stem.

Determine the standards required

For each job under your control you should determine the standards of performance required. Include the required responsibilities and competencies in the job description and job specification. Explain to each employee exactly what is expected from their position. Agree these standards with each of the individuals involved. Then do everything you can to help your people develop to the required standard.

Coach

Coach the individual members of your team in order to develop their skills and level of competence. Coaching begins with explaining exactly what needs to be done. You then show the person how to do the task. You then monitor and observe. When they return the completed work you can review it with them and point out areas where they can improve or develop. This constructive feedback helps them to develop their skills. You need to let the person practise repetitive tasks until they form a level of expertise. Finally you can help the person to manage their own learning by pointing them in the right direction and giving suggestions on how they can acquire additional knowledge. Your aim is to get your people to think for themselves and to make their own decisions.

Give additional responsibility

The best way to develop people is to give them additional responsibility. Build up their level of responsibility in a gradual manner. Every time you delegate a new task you are helping to develop the person involved. Allow your employees to develop their skills through taking on additional obligations. Give progressively less guidance as they learn to deal with issues themselves. Eventually your role as coach will involve less training and will become a matter of letting them discover things for themselves. Your people will eventually outstrip your abilities in many areas. At this stage you are developing the leaders of the future.

Let them make mistakes

The only way for people to learn is to make mistakes. Mistakes are an integral part of the learning process. If you are going to develop your people then you must assign them new and unfamiliar tasks. When you do so, they will make mistakes at first. Your job is to be tolerant and accept this. You should offer praise and encouragement for what they have achieved. You then must offer constructive guidance on how they can improve next time. Accept that performance will improve with experience.

Accept their limitations

Accept the limitations of your team members. Everyone has different talents and abilities. While you can help individuals develop, this will take time and resources. Delegate the work according to the abilities of the individual concerned.

Set challenging targets

If you want to develop your people, then set progressively more challenging targets and watch them grow in confidence and ability.

Provide constructive feedback

Providing regular constructive feedback will help to change behaviour and perspectives. You must provide feedback in private. You must be specific and focus on the behaviour rather than the person. Point out what is missing from the performance or the thinking of the individual. Deal with issues as soon as possible, but wait until emotions have had a chance to settle. Listen to the reasons offered for the behaviour, there may have been mitigating circumstances.

Measure and review performance

Measure the performance of each team member. Review this regularly with each person involved. Allow for a learning curve. People will improve with practise and experience. Their performance will improve with time. Point out where any gaps can be closed, so that individual targets are met.

Lead by example

Set an example for others to follow. Your team will pay more attention to your words if they are backed up with your actions.

Job enlargement

Review the training requirements for each individual in your team in order to develop them. Give them different tasks to carry out. This adds variety to their work. Allow them to be involved in more of the process. Rotate the work you delegate amongst different team members to achieve this result. Let them understand the relevance and importance of their role. They must understand the difference their job makes to the organisation. Everyone wants to be valued and appreciated.

Job enrichment

Give your employees additional authority, autonomy and control over their job functions. Involve them in the setting of their own targets and performance standards. Give them more scope to plan, act, monitor performance and take corrective action. Let them develop their own solutions to problems.

Personal growth

Allow individuals the opportunity for personal growth by providing training to upgrade skills and progress their careers. Encourage each individual to draw up a personal development plan.

Chapter 14. Strengthening your team

From time to time you will need to strengthen your time by hiring replacements or additional help. You will need to assess interview candidates based on a number of criteria. You should look to hire someone with the right qualities and attitude, even if they are lacking some experience. It is easier to provide the opportunity to gain the additional experience than it is to change someone's attitudes.

You should assess candidates on their:

- Skill level and competency.
- Willingness to work hard and exceed targets.
- A proactive approach.
- Work experience.
- Matching competencies in terms of the job requirements.
- Previous achievements.
- Commitment to developing their career.
- Full understanding of the implications of doing the job.
- Ability to do the job.
- Ability to learn new tasks.
- Willingness to persevere and overcome difficulties.
- Ability to work well under pressure.
- Ability to meet deadlines.
- Ability to work unsupervised.
- Ability to set goals and willingness to follow through on them.
- Ability to solve problems.
- Willingness to show initiative.
- Tendency to set personal goals and review performance.

- Evidence of learning from mistakes.
- Reliability.
- Ability to add value to the organisation.
- Evidence that the job is the candidate's clear first choice.
- Level of enthusiasm.
- Level of motivation.
- Commitment to the role.
- Attention to detail.
- Suitability for the role.
- Compatibility with corporate ethos.
- Positive response to instructions and authority.
- Ability to build and maintain relationships with work colleagues.
- Ability to adapt to changing work conditions.
- Probability that they will remain with the company.
- Any discrepancy between answers.
- Signs that they are hiding anything.
- Signs of any negative traits that would exclude them.

Chapter 15. Assertiveness

Be assertive

A leader must learn to be assertive. Assertive behaviour involves standing up for your own rights while respecting the rights of others. Assertive behaviour is not the same as aggressive behaviour, which involves violating or ignoring the rights of others. It is not the same as passive behaviour, where a person acts in a subservient manner.

Avoid aggressive behaviour

Do not use aggressive behaviour when dealing with others. There are two probable outcomes when using aggressive behaviour, neither of which is constructive. Aggressive behaviour can promote an aggressive response, particularly from peers or more senior colleagues. The issue then escalates into an argument and conflict. If you use aggressive behaviour with subordinates you will end up with a team that is demoralised and dissatisfied. Your employees will become resentful and withdrawn and will only act when instructed to do so.

Avoid passive behaviour

The problem with passive behaviour is that it leads others to take advantage of you. They will also lose respect for you. They will delegate work to you that they do not want to do themselves. You should avoid passive, submissive behaviour. You are not a doormat. As a leader you must respect your needs equally to the needs of others.

Dealing with aggressive people

Do not adapt a passive behaviour pattern if you are confronted with aggressive demands from others. Remain calm, and increase the level of your assertiveness. Stick to the facts and the issues. You must stand your ground.

How to behave in an assertive manner

Assertive behaviour enables leaders to influence others. Believe in yourself and express these beliefs confidently. As a leader you should behave in the following manner:

- Speak briefly and to the point.
- Specify exactly the outcome you require.
- Indicate that you are speaking for yourself.
- Make your own decisions.
- Do not let others talk down to you.
- Accept that you are equal to others.
- Defend your rights, without violating the rights of others.
- Acknowledge that others have different opinions.
- Treat yourself and others with equal respect.
- Be responsible for your own actions and decisions.
- Specify your stance or position.
- Repeat your position if required.
- Point out the consequences of inappropriate behaviour in others.

Chapter 16. Delegating

Your job as coach

As a leader your time should be spent setting goals and objectives, planning the course of action, instructing, coaching and motivating others and reviewing performance and progress. You are no longer a team player, you are the coach. It is the responsibility of your team to carry out the required action. Your job is to get the most from your team. If they win, then you win. You cannot become an additional player and coach at the same time. If you attempt to do this you will fail. You will not have the time to do everything.

Value your time

Your time must be spent on your primary objective of leading others. Keep this in mind when reviewing everything that needs to be done. When you list everything that needs to be done you must prioritise the work depending on the urgency and the importance. If a task is neither urgent nor important then question if it needs to be done at all.

Having prioritised tasks you must decide what to delegate. The answer is simple. Delegate everything that you possibly can. Never do anything that someone else can do for you. Why hire and develop talented people if you are going to hold on to the work yourself? Reserve your time exclusively for leading others and carrying out core activities that will move you closer to achieving your personal goals. Treat everything else as a distraction that needs to be dropped or delegated.

Effective delegation improves your performance as a leader. It frees you up from routine and less critical tasks. It allows you to concentrate on more important work. It allows you to think about medium and longer term strategy.

Delegating work motivates and develops your team. It also speeds up the decision making process by allowing them to take control of their own actions.

Authority

When delegating tasks you can also delegate the authority to make decisions and control the process.

Responsibility

Responsibility is the obligation to complete a task assigned to you by higher authority. The responsibility remains with you and cannot be delegated. You can, however, delegate the task.

Accountability

Accountability involves being answerable for the outcome of a task. If the task fails to be completed properly or on time then accountability is where the finger of blame will point. Accountability cannot be delegated.

How to delegate effectively

There is a difference between delegation and abdication. If you choose to delegate work that is within your remit you will still be held accountable and responsible for it. It is therefore in your interest to take care to delegate all tasks properly. This will ensure that they are carried out on time and to the required standard. To do this you must:

- Set the priorities.
- Decide on what should be delegated.
- Decide who is best suited for each task.
- Attempt to assign only one person per task.
- Brief the person properly by explaining the task.
- Give a brief reason for needing the task completed.
- Give an indication of the importance of the task.
- Define the specific objectives.
- Define the authority level being delegated.
- Base this authority on the requirements of the task.
- Set any deadlines and targets.
- Offer support and encouragement.
- Ensure that the person understands what needs to be done.
- Get the person to confirm willingness and ability to complete the task.
- Provide adequate resources to get the job done.
- Let the person get on with the task without undue interference.
- Let them choose their own methods of getting the job completed.
- Do not micromanage.
- Provide adequate guidance and supervision.
- Check on progress and results at agreed intervals.
- Check the critical issues.
- Encourage your team to report any problems or difficulties promptly.
- Encourage your team to seek advice as required.
- Gradually increase the level of authority to make their own decisions.
- Evaluate the final results.

- Thank, praise and reward your subordinates as appropriate.
- Provide positive, constructive feedback on any areas that could have been tackled better.

Why you should delegate

- It will reduce your personal workload.
- It will increase the free time that you have available.
- It will increase your productivity.
- It will enable you to complete more tasks.
- It will free you up to concentrate on the important issues.
- It will give you more time to plan and supervise.
- It will allow you to specialise.
- It will allow you to take the longer term view.
- It will develop your team.
- It will motivate your team.
- It will increase the responsibility of your team.
- It will help to build trust and belief.
- It will foster collaboration and team spirit.
- It will help in the assessment of your team members.
- Your team is better than you at completing the tasks.
- It will improve your work-life balance.
- It will enable your work to continue, even when you are not there.

What to delegate

- Anything that you do not need to do yourself.
- Any task that should be completed by someone less qualified.
- Anything that others can do faster or better.
- Routine and repetitive tasks.
- Tasks that are time consuming.
- Anything that can help to develop your team.

- Interesting and challenging tasks to help motivate your team.
- Entire tasks that provide a sense of achievement.
- Specialist tasks to those with the skills and experience to complete them.

Things you should delegate that people tend not to

As a leader you must delegate as much as you possibly can to your team. Many people are reluctant to delegate certain categories of tasks. They continue to carry out activities that do not contribute to their goals. They do not delegate:

- Tasks that they deem to be important.
- Tasks that they are best at completing.
- Tasks that they are quickest at completing.
- Shorter tasks.

You may have built up an expertise at completing a task. However if you delegate it to someone else he will eventually become equally adept at completing it. Even if a task is important, it does not mean that you are the best person to do it. If it does not contribute to your long term personal goals, then let a member of your team complete it.

When to delegate

- When you have established your priorities.
- When you cannot allocate sufficient time to do it yourself.
- When deadlines are approaching.
- When you need to keep subordinates occupied.
- When you would like a different viewpoint on a problem.

- When you want to develop subordinates.

When *not* to delegate

- When you have been specifically instructed to complete the task yourself.
- When your subordinate is already overloaded.
- When your subordinate lacks the necessary skills and experience.
- As a means of punishment.
- When the task is doomed to fail from the outset.
- When the information is of a confidential nature.

Fear of delegating

Some people are afraid to delegate tasks because they:

- Lack the necessary confidence and trust in their subordinates.
- Are afraid that the task will not be completed to the required standard.
- Do not want to lose control.
- Worry that it will take as long to explain the task as it would to do it themselves.
- Take satisfaction in completing the task themselves.
- Wish to appear busy.
- Do not want to overload others.
- Do not wish to be accused of dumping unwanted tasks onto others.
- Are afraid that they will have to repeat the task themselves.
- Are afraid that their subordinate might outshine them.
- Cannot find anyone immediately available to carry out the task.
- Do not want to be continually interrupted to help

with the task.

These reasons are simply excuses for holding onto the familiar. A person who does not delegate is often more afraid of replacing the task with something new and unfamiliar. They would rather remain in their comfort zone than take on additional responsibilities.

Symptoms of poor delegation

It is easy to recognise a working environment where there is a lack of proper delegation. The leader will be overloaded, stressed, continually at his desk and unavailable to his subordinates. The subordinates will not be fully utilised. They will be bored and lack motivation. When they are assigned work there will be a tendency to micromanage the work. Deadlines will be missed. There will be a general lack of direction and control. There will be excessive turnover. The team members will need to seek authority for routine decisions and there will be unnecessary interference in their routine tasks.

Choosing who should do the work

When delegating a task you should choose the person who has the knowledge, skills, motivation and available time to complete the task properly. Match the complexity of the task with the experience of the chosen team member. Try to give people tasks that will stretch them a little and help them to develop. Do not give the task to someone who does not have adequate skills or experience. Do not simply give the task to the first person you encounter. Think about the task and how the allocation will benefit the person involved. Do not give all of the challenging and rewarding tasks to your favourite subordinate.

Delegating different levels of authority

Delegation levels vary from retaining complete control to fully relinquishing the task. You must decide which level is appropriate based on the complexity of the task and the experience of the individual team member involved.

Level 1. Follow the exact instructions

At this level you instruct your subordinate on the exact action to take. You retain total control. You do not delegate any authority. You issue clear instructions, rules and guidelines. You tell the person exactly how they should carry out the task. You retain authority for all of the decision making process. You might delegate in this manner to an inexperienced subordinate who is tackling a new problem for the first time.

Level 2. Research and report back

At this level you give specific instructions, but provide scope to investigate the problem and report back on any issues. You make the decisions and issue any additional instructions. You would delegate this level of authority to a member of the team with experience in tackling similar problems.

Level 3. Research and make suggestions.

At this level you brief the subordinate and allow him to investigate and suggest possible solutions. You ask for details on the issue, suggestions for action and the reasoning behind any proposals. You retain responsibility for any decision making. You would delegate this level of authority to an experienced subordinate tackling an unfamiliar or complex task.

Level 4. make the decisions, but keep me informed

At this level you are delegating almost complete control. You give general directions to your subordinate and ask for feedback at his discretion. You trust your subordinate to make the decisions. Your main concern is that the project stays on schedule. You would delegate this level of authority to an experienced team member tackling a complex issue with which they are familiar.

Level 5. Look after this yourself

At this level you decide to delegate the task permanently to your subordinate. It becomes part of their duties. They are empowered to take whatever action is required. They can even choose to delegate it themselves. You just need the task to be completed on time and to specification. How they do this is their concern.

Keep track of delegated tasks

Keep a log of the tasks you delegated. Record who you delegated the task to and the expected completion date. Use the log to help monitor progress.

Do not micromanage

You must learn to let go once you have delegated a task. Do not micromanage. Trust your team to get on with their work. Just make yourself available to deal with any issues that they may encounter. If you stand over a person while they are completing a task you will simply demoralise and de-motivate them. Get on with your own work and free your staff to express themselves. Allow them to gain experience from learning from their own mistakes.

Chapter 17. Time management

Advantages of managing your time

Effective time management will:

- Simplify your job and life.
- Reduce your stress levels.
- Increase your effectiveness.
- Increase your efficiency.
- Increase your job satisfaction.
- Increase your team's productivity.
- Improve your work-life balance.
- Help secure your next promotion.

Time is a limited resource

Time is a finite resource. Time is limited and precious. As a leader you cannot add to the total time available to you. You are limited to 24 hours a day like everyone else. Once the time is gone you can never get it back. What you must do is make the most of the time you have available.

You should be able to complete your work in about 40 hours each week. If you cannot manage this then you are doing something wrong. If you choose to work longer each week it should be to further your long term personal goals through study or other work.

Taking an overall view

To make the best use of your limited time you must first step back and take an overall view. Look at your job description and think about what you are meant to achieve. Set your overall objectives with your boss. Think about your own long term personal career objectives. Where do you want to end your career? Now look at the steps required to get you there. Look at what is preventing you from getting your next promotion. What qualifications and experience do you need to acquire? What objectives do your team need to hit to get you there? Now set out a three year plan that will get you that promotion. Set milestones and target dates along the way.

Setting priorities

You need to determine how to set priorities at work. Every task that you receive needs to be evaluated and prioritised. Some tasks that are not important need to be dropped or refused. You then need to schedule and delegate the tasks. Pareto's analysis states that 80% of the gains are made from 20% of the activity. Your methodology should be to concentrate on the important 20% of tasks that yield 80% of the benefits.

The importance of a task

Every task that comes across your desk needs to be judged in terms of your personal career goals. Will the task contribute to your career goals? If so it is important, if not it is not as important. Consider the benefits of carrying out the task. What are the gains likely to be? Look at the consequences of not carrying out the task. If these are low then the task is unimportant and might possibly be dropped. Is the task one in which you will be judged against your performance objectives by your boss? If so then it is important. Is the task interdependent on other tasks?

Will other important tasks be delayed if this task is not completed? If so you will need to treat the task as being important.

The urgency of a task

The urgency of a task is a function of its deadline. As the deadline approaches a task becomes more urgent. If the task is holding up other tasks it will also be regarded as urgent. Beware of the urgency of tasks. Tasks usually become urgent because they were not properly foreseen, planned and prioritised in the first place.

How to prioritise tasks

If a task is urgent and important, then it needs to be done right away. Look to delegate it if at all possible.

About 50% of the tasks will be important, but not urgent. You should look to spend as much time as possible completing important tasks. It is possible to schedule important, non urgent, tasks for later and assign someone to whom they can be delegated.

Minimise urgent tasks

Make sure that tasks are completed in a timely fashion in advance of deadlines. If you continually allow tasks to become urgent then the working environment will become stressed.

Many tasks are urgent, but not important. They often come as requests from someone else who has failed to manage their own time. Turn these requests down if possible. While important to the other person, they do not form part of your remit. They will prevent you from being efficient in carrying out your own important tasks. If you cannot turn them down then look to renegotiate the deadline. People often ask for tasks to be completed sooner than they actually require them. They are building in a safety factor in case you do not deliver on time.

Drop unimportant tasks

Finally about 25% of the tasks will be unimportant and really just a distraction. Make sure that all of this work is dropped. It does not add value. It does not contribute towards your goals. It will only lead to inefficiency. Question how things are done. Question the need for reports and meetings. Question the need for procedures and policies. Look at how things can be simplified.

Keep an activity log

Keep an activity log of how you spend your time. This might just be a matter of jotting down in your diary in half hour segments exactly what you are engaged in during the day. Review this activity log after two weeks to get a feeling for how you are spending your time. Look to reduce time spent on:

- Unimportant tasks
- Interruptions
- Delays
- Work that should have been delegated.
- Dealing with e-mails.
- Reacting to crisis situations.
- Travelling.

Try to maximise your time spent on core, important tasks that contribute to achieving your goals. Eliminate everything that is unnecessary and unimportant.

Time management tips

In order to manage your time you should:

- Set clear goals for yourself and your team.
- Keep a list of things to do.
- Plan and prioritise your objectives.
- Use marginal time.
- Use tools such as a diary, personal organizer and calendars.
- Set realistic time limits on tasks.
- Set deadlines and target to be early.
- Concentrate on one thing at a time.
- Stick to your schedule.
- Break larger tasks down into smaller tasks.
- Delegate as much as you can.
- Avoid distraction and interruptions.
- Become proactive.
- Do not procrastinate.
- Only check e-mails twice per day.
- Remove yourself from unwanted distribution lists.
- De-clutter your desk and office.
- Screen unwanted visitors.
- Reserve blocks of time when you will not be interrupted.
- Manage meetings effectively.
- Bin irrelevant information.
- Read summaries rather than the full report.
- Question the need for meetings.
- Learn to say no.
- Cut out unnecessary processes, methods, procedures,

correspondence and paperwork.
- Use out of office auto-replies for e-mails.
- Clear in-trays and e-mail in boxes every day.
- Avoid unnecessary travel.

Chapter 18. Persuading

Understanding others

Leaders need to be emotionally intelligent. They must be self-aware. They must understand the need to influence and empathise with others and build relationships. People are emotional beings as well as rational ones. If you are to get the best from people you must first understand their personalities and listen to their concerns.

Long term influence

In order to influence the behaviour of others you must actively listen to their viewpoint and concerns. You must display empathy for their position. You must support them in their areas of primary concern. You must build rapport. You must gain their trust. Only then can you hope to influence them and begin to change their behaviour. If you do not understand people and have not listened to their concerns there is no way that you can possibly gain their trust and hope to alter their behaviour.

Integrity and influence

Maintain integrity in everything you do. Set high standards of behaviour and professionalism in your dealings with others. Build a reputation for integrity. Integrity breeds trust and trust brings support and additional business. Actions speak louder than words. People will judge you on your behaviour rather than on your words.

Dress to impress

Your appearance needs to be right if you are trying to sell an idea or a product to someone. You need to be well groomed and attired. As a general rule always dress for the job you want, not the one you have. People will judge you on your first impression and that is your appearance. They will have formed an opinion on you before you even open your mouth. So make sure that your appearance is professional.

Act with confidence

Carry yourself with confidence. Stand up straight, keep your shoulders back and remain calm and composed. Look and behave like you are successful and people will accept that you are. If you show any signs of self doubt people will not buy into the message that you are sending.

Make a connection

When you first meet people you need to make a connection. To do this make eye contact, smile and give a friendly greeting. Remain polite and ask a question that shows general interest.

Be positive in outlook

You need to adapt and maintain the correct mental attitude at all times. If you are positive in outlook it will be easier to attract others to your cause. If you radiate positive energy people will congregate around you like moths around a light source. Remain cheerful, upbeat and optimistic. It is the best way to attract support from others.

Banish all negative vocabulary and body language

from your persona. This only turns people off. Concentrate on solutions not problems.

Express optimism and enthusiasm

Express optimism and enthusiasm for all of your ideas. This is often enough to convince others to want to get involved.

Address people by their name

Address people by their name. Everyone likes to be treated as an individual. The best way to do this is to use their name. If you use someone's name you automatically get their attention.

Shake hands

Most people will advise you on the importance of a firm handshake while maintaining eye contact. One other technique you can employ is to hold the grip just a few seconds longer and ask the other person how they are feeling. You are enforcing the message that you are pleased to meet them and that you care about them.

Compliment people

When you meet people find some little thing to compliment them about. Then immediately ask their opinion on something. So you could say "I love your watch. What did you think of the last presentation?"

Talk about their favourite subject

When you meet people talk initially about their favourite subject. This will invariably be themselves, their children or their hobbies. Listen to what is said and ask them follow up questions. Build rapport with them. The next time you meet this person, return to their favourite topic. This shows that you have been listening and that you care about them as an individual.

Take an interest in people and they will take an interest in you. You will find it easier to do business with them. They will be more receptive to suggestions. They will impart more information. They will become loyal customers.

Be aware of people's expectations

Be aware of what people expect to get from an encounter. You can use this to your advantage. You may have to alter their expectations, but you must be aware of what they are. Ask questions early on in your conversation to determine their expectations. You can then reinforce that you are meeting their expectations by selling them your concept or product.

Keep the message simple

Keep your message simple and easy to understand. Keep it concise and clear. Avoid long complicated sentences or phrases. Avoid high brow content. Avoid technical terminology. Avoid vague references, abstract allusions or innuendo. All of these are barriers to understanding. Say what you mean and mean what you say.

Get to the point

Get to the point quickly and state the crux of the matter. People are busy. They are preoccupied with their own concerns. Do not ramble on or you will lose their attention. The quicker you get to your point the better it will be received by your audience.

Repeat the message

The best way to reinforce a message is to find ways of repeating it. The more you repeat, the more the message gets through. If you are selling an idea, then repeat the benefits in different ways. Compliance comes with repetition of the request. The more you ask, the more likely the answer will be yes.

What's in it for them?

Quickly show the other person what they can gain from your proposals. Explain what it means to them and why it is important to them. This is the fastest and easiest way for you to gain their support. Most people only want to know what is in it for them. They are not interested in your concerns. They are working to their own agenda. People are either looking to gain something from your proposal or they wish to avoid losing something. Pitch your sale accordingly.

If you are selling a product to someone you should talk about the benefits it will bring, not the features it possesses. People only want a product if it can bring benefit to them. A product can have dozens of features, but the customer will not buy it if he cannot see the benefit.

Prevent them from losing

People have a great fear of losing things. They want to retain what they already have. It is more important for

them to hold onto what they already have than to gain
something new. So point out what they could lose,
then show them how your proposal will let them hold
onto it. The more important the thing is to them the
more they will buy into your proposal.

Credit the idea to someone else

You can credit the idea to someone else in order to
break down barriers to acceptance. You can say
something like "My father once told me that....."
Alternatively try something like "A wise man once
told me that...." This adds credibility to what you are
proposing as it is now coming from multiple sources.

Offer them a choice

Offer people a choice of options, any of which are
acceptable to you. This way you get agreement on at
least one course of action that you favour.

Ask for their help

If you ask a colleague for help without specifying
what you want it often results in a tacit commitment
before you start. They would like to help. They just
don't want you taking up too much of their time or
resources. So if what you ask for is less than what they
feared they will be relieved and agree right way.

Tell a story

Use stories to illustrate your points. Stories paint
pictures in people's minds. It helps them visualize the
concept. People find stories easy to follow and
understand. People relate to stories. People remember

stories. Some of the greatest orators of all time used stories and metaphors to illustrate their point. The teachings of Socrates and Jesus Christ are laden with storytelling and metaphor.

Speak their language

Talk to people in a language that they can understand. Listen to their metaphors and use them to relate to their concerns. Echo their values and beliefs. Talk about their interests and concerns. By relating to people you can gain their interest.

Give rather than take

If you want to get what you want, the best way to do this is to offer something else first. People feel obliged to respond in kind when someone gives them something.

Let them think it was their idea

You can convince people with your arguments, but it is easier to persuade them with their own ideas. People will doubt what you tell them, but they will never doubt what they have concluded for themselves. If it is their idea, you do not need to sell it to them. People will always support a cause if they believe that it was their idea in the first place. Indirect suggestion can be achieved in a number of ways. You can simply prompt someone by raising an issue and asking for advice and suggestions. Then focus in on the suggestion that supports your desired course of action. The fact that it was the other person's suggestion will be enough to gain their support.

Make them a confidant

If you begin a conversation with "I shouldn't tell you this, but.." you will instantly grab someone's attention. You are making them a confidant in your secret insight that others are being excluded from. You are appealing to their sense of belonging.

Distance yourself from the idea

If you use denial it distances you from the message and makes it easier to buy into the concept. So you can begin by saying "I am not saying that you should do this, but most people like to ....." In this case you are denying the suggestion, while appealing to the herd concept. The other person will want to experience what everyone else is doing.

Let them persuade you

You are probably aware of people who continually like to take the opposite stance from any proposal that is made. Why not try an alternative approach? Get them to persuade you to take the desired course of action. You could say that you were thinking of a certain course of action but the time does not seem right and the budgets are tight and maybe it's not a good idea.

Once you have framed it this way they will behave as they always do by assuming the polar opposite. They will think of loads of good ideas why everyone should proceed on this course. You just need to show some reluctance and then finally capitulate to their 'ideas'.

Remind them of past favours

If someone does not respond in a positive manner to your requests you could remind them of a past favour that you did for them.

Ask rather than tell

You will elicit more support when you ask for a favour, rather than issuing an instruction. There is a subtle difference between the two. Obviously when the employee is part of your team they must follow the instructions. However, it is nicer to be asked in a polite manner rather than to be on the receiving end of a brusque ultimatum.

Be consistent

Be consistent in the language of your communication. You must be confident and decisive if you want others to go along with your suggestion. Any sign of doubt on your part and you will not gain support.

Pick the right moment

Pick the right moment to make a request. Study the body language of the other person and gauge their mood before you make a request. You are more likely to succeed in your request if the other person is in a good mood and receptive. Do not make your request if they are preoccupied with other concerns.

Offer praise

If you offer praise and confidence in the other person's abilities they are more likely to help you out.

Offer a reward

You could offer a small reward in return for a favour.

Promise to return the favour

You could try offering to return the favour at some point in the future.

Thank people

Thank people for their help and support. Don't just say the words, "Thank you." Add a little comment about how much you appreciate it and how generous, kind or considerate they have been. Then watch the difference your response makes.

Thank people in person and in writing. Reciprocate by returning the favour. Build on any friendship or alliance that this will foster.

Publicly acknowledge contribution

If someone does help out with a proposal or project then publicly acknowledge that commitment. This will make them more inclined to help out in future. It will also help members of the audience to consider helping you in future endeavours.

Bridging

Draw out the other person's point of view. Acknowledge and agree with what you can, then try to bridge their views with your own. Let them negotiate and shape your proposals as long as you get your bottom line requirements.

Reason

You can apply reason to an argument in order to influence the other party. You may decide to back up your argument with supporting facts and figures. Relate your proposals to studies, research or expert viewpoints. Rather than using emotional appeal you are relying on objective information to prove your case. This adds to the legitimacy of your case.

Assertiveness

If you have more power than the other person, you may choose to simply be assertive and tell the other person to follow your instructions. If they are reluctant you can simply point out the rules and regulations. While this method will work you should use it as an option of last resort.

Upward referral

You might use this strategy with a peer. You could say that your boss wanted all of his direct reports to carry out the desired action.

Form and alliance

Consider the merits of forming an alliance with a like thinking individual in order to push through a proposal. Look at shared concerns and develop an explicit agreement on a combined course of action. The other person may have more influence with others whom you would like to enlist in your proposal.

Choose your seat

Sit alongside someone rather than directly opposite if you want to gain their consent. By sitting opposite you are taking up a confrontational position.

Divide and conquer

You can talk to each individual member of a group in isolation if you need to overcome resistance from them all. This way you can win them over one at a time. However think about the issues. If everyone else thinks a different course of action is correct then you need to take time to reflect. Perhaps there is merit in what they believe, particularly if the group is closer to the job than you are. If you are still convinced that your proposal is correct then you must make sure that you clearly explain the logic in your approach.

Chapter 19. Negotiating

The negotiating process

Leaders will be called upon to negotiate from time to time. You may have to negotiate a better salary for yourself. You may need to negotiate a budget for your area or better resources for your team. You may need to negotiate with customers or with suppliers. Whatever the circumstances you must realise that you get very little in this life without asking for it. If you want a better deal you need to be prepared to ask for it. No one else is going to do it for you.

Negotiations involve a conflict of interests. The negotiating process involves an atmosphere of uncertainty from the outset. Neither side knows what the other side is prepared to settle for. The outcome is unknown and uncertain.

Negotiations follow a familiar pattern. One side makes an opening offer. This will be less than they are willing to concede. The other side then asks for more than they hope to get. The haggling begins. Eventually both sides meet somewhere in the middle. This is known as a win-win situation. Both parties are content to walk away with something from the deal.

Rules of the negotiating game

The one rule that you must appreciate about negotiating is that anything goes. You will be confronted with negativity, obstinacy and resistance. That is the nature of the negotiating game. Both sides take part in a form of role play. Both sides are attempting to gain as much as possible from the deal.

Do not expect the other side to play fair. You will not be treated with kid gloves. The other side will cry poverty. They will offer as little as possible. They will talk about limited budgets. They will question your figures and research. They will say that you have over priced yourself. They will claim that they cannot afford your demands. They will hint at cheaper alternatives elsewhere. They will attempt to undermine your credibility. They will do their best to wear you down.

They will attempt to put you under pressure. They will put a time limit on any offer. They will threaten to withdraw their interim offer. They will try all of these tactics and more. The aim is to force you into accepting an offer on their terms. They will do anything and everything to get you to sign up, as soon as possible, for as little as possible.

As far as negotiations are concerned, you do not get what you deserve. You get what you are prepared to negotiate. This might seem unfair to you. However the other party has a business to run. To do this they must maximise profits. One way of doing this is to minimise total costs, which includes whatever they need to pay you for your service or products.

Your negotiating strategy

- Carry out market research in advance and work out the probable value of your offering.
- Carry out thorough research on the other negotiating party. Talk to people who have negotiated with them and find out the tactics they employ.
- Know your ideal goal, your likely target and your

bottom line.

- Prepare your offering as a package so that you can trade concessions on different items.

- Ask for more than you want. They will be bidding you downwards.

- Do not be specific on your demands. Quote a range if needs be.

- Be prepared to justify your positioning.

- Let the other side do the talking. Let them take the driving seat. The less you say the better. If you talk they will pick holes in your argument. By not talking you can read their signals and body language. Concentrate on what the other side is implying, as well as the actual spoken words.

- Know your worth and what you can contribute in terms of benefits.

- Be firm. Outline your needs, but don't issue demands and ultimatums. Remain professional and courteous throughout. Do not lock them into a position that they cannot accept.

- Do not take things personally. Keep the conversation light hearted. Smile, be friendly and break the ice when you can. Avoid confrontation, which forces people into entrenched positions.

- Try to establish where they are more likely to be flexible.

- You can negotiate more if you are willing and able to walk away from a deal.

- Listen carefully. The other side will give reasons for their objections. These reasons never apply to all aspects of any proposal. Not being able to move on one aspect, does not imply that they are hampered in a similar manner elsewhere.

- Be prepared to make concessions at the latter stages of the process. Pick something that is less important to you. Hinting that you are willing to make a concession may be enough to get the other side to reciprocate. By trading concessions you may get what you want.

Do not name your price

Do not name your price. Let the other side make the opening offer. Whoever makes the opening offer will be negotiating from a position of weakness. Initial offers define one limit of the negotiating zone. If the other side makes an initial offer then this becomes your lower limit. This is your safety net. They cannot reduce this opening offer. You can negotiate upwards on this lower limit. You have the impetus and something to aim for. You are in control.

If you make the opening demand, this immediately becomes the upper limit. You have declared your hand. You can only go downwards. The problem is that you do not know how low you will be forced. You have no safety net. You do not know what the other side will offer. You have handed them the initiative and control over the process. They will now offer as little as possible. You have an uphill battle to get anywhere near your needs.

The opening bid

- When the other side make an opening bid you should remain silent for as long as possible and look disappointed.
- Never concede anything at the opening stage, or your case will collapse.

The bargaining process

- Keep calm and do not display emotions. A low initial

offer is what you should expect and what you will get. It is not an estimate of your worth.

- Bid them upwards. Say that you expected a better offer. Do not specify your requirements. Ask them to improve on their offer.
- Make conditional proposals.
- Do not make one sided concessions. Trade off for something in return.
- Hint at your reluctance to do business elsewhere.
- Be patient. Do not appear anxious to secure a deal.
- Negotiate on the whole package. Do not let the other side pick off concessions one at a time.
- If you are getting nowhere on price, then negotiate on the other terms.
- Do not let the other side put a time pressure on you to sign any deal.

Close the deal

Once you have got what you want on your main terms you should concede a minor point to show flexibility. This allows for a win-win situation. Be prepared to move from your opening position. This will allow the other side to feel that they have got something from the negotiations.

Failure to agree

Be prepared to walk away if they cannot meet your minimum requirements.

Negotiation pitfalls you should avoid

- Lack of research in advance.
- Settling for the initial offer.
- Turning down an offer immediately, instead of

negotiating a better deal.
- Producing a list of demands.
- Making the opening bid.
- Talking too much.
- Aiming too low. Not asking for more than you want.
- Revealing your bottom line early in negotiations.
- Focusing on your requirements rather than on what you can contribute.
- Not being assertive enough.
- Becoming emotionally involved.
- Being aggressive or adversarial.
- Issuing ultimatums or drawing a line in the sand.
- Appearing anxious to settle.

Chapter 20. Managing conflict

Conflict in organisations

A leader must be able to deal with conflict. Wherever you have humans you will get conflict. The workplace is no exception. Organisations are set up for rivalry and conflict. Organisations consist of different departments, which inevitably become competing tribes. This happens because of limited budgets, salaries and promotion opportunities. The combined needs of the individual parts of the organisation always exceed the limited total resources that are available. Managers in each area can become embroiled in conflict as they compete for limited resources or the attention of senior management. Everyone wants their fair share of the cake.

The cost of destructive conflict

Conflict can be destructive. Conflict imposes costs on the organisation and the individuals involved. Conflict can hinder co-operative action. These costs include delayed and poor decision making, lost productivity, stress, lost time and poor morale. When people lose out as a result of conflict they feel dissatisfied, defeated, de-motivated, demoralised and dejected. They retreat into their own camps. The conflict accentuates the differences between individuals or groups. There is distrust, suspicion and ill-will. People can even harbour feelings of revenge.

Types of conflict

Conflict may arise in a number of different areas. As a leader you will have to deal with the conflict as it arises:

- Between your team and another team.
- Between yourself and your boss.
- Between yourself and a member of your team.
- Between different members of your team.
- Between yourself and your peers.
- Between yourself and a customer.
- Between yourself and a supplier.

Causes of conflict

Conflict can be caused by a number of initiating factors. It is important for a leader to recognise the possible contributing factors and to remove these from the work environment.

- Poorly defined goals.
- Conflicting goals.
- Poorly defined roles.
- Environmental stress.
- Competition.
- Limited resources.
- Differences of opinion.
- Inadequate communication.
- Inadequate information.
- Poor listening skills.
- Incompatibility of roles.
- Poor co-operation.
- Disagreement on facts, goals, methods or values.
- Threatening or aggressive behaviour.

Definition of roles

It is important to clearly define roles in order to avoid unnecessary conflict. Every member of your team should clearly understand their role and that of the other team members. They must understand who is responsible for carrying out each task. If their roles are interdependent, then the boundaries need to be clearly defined. They should understand how you expect them to collaborate. They should know what to do if differences of opinion occur. The expected outcome and operating procedures should be clearly specified.

Communication

Lack of communication is one of the major underlying causes of conflict. Unclear goals and targets and hidden agendas can lead to mistrust, duplication of effort and division.

Misunderstanding

Misunderstanding is often the root cause of conflict. It often occurs due to a lack of communication. People can come to the wrong conclusions if there is insufficient communication.

Emotions

Emotions are often based on how people perceive that they have been treated. Emotions may not actually be based on factual events. Emotional conflict can continue even when the cause of the initial disagreement has been resolved.

Viewpoints

Conflict can arise out of different viewpoints. Different departments have different perspectives and priorities, which may often be in conflict with one another.

Values

Conflict can arise out of a difference in values or fundamental beliefs.

Build trust and openness

By holding regular team meetings you can encourage team members to air their views and feelings. This should get any issues out in the open where they can be dealt with in a constructive manner.

Do not become involved in conflict

Do not be drawn into a conflict situation. Do not react to provocation. Do not apportion blame. Remain positive. Focus on the desired outcome. Do not bear a grudge. Remember that it is better to win a friend than an argument.

Conflict resolution

Leaders must be able to retract people from entrenched positions. Leaders must be able to mediate. Leaders must be able to get both parties to a conflict to agree on common ground and a common challenge. This common ground might be the overall aims of the organisation, such as growth or profitability. Both parties must be able to save face and be seen to gain something from the dispute. There is a need for a win/win outcome.

Deal with conflict early

You need to be aware and watch out for the early signs of tension. Look out for differing viewpoints that can lead to conflict. Deal immediately with the first signs of conflict. Do not avoid dealing with conflict, in the hope that the issue will resolve itself. This is an abdication of your responsibilities. Do not let hostilities fester. Matters will only get worse.

Deal with the issues

The most important thing to realise when dealing with conflict is that you must stick to the issues. You should separate all emotion and personalities from the issues. Accept that people are different. Recognise that people have different perceptions. Do not show personal bias. Deal with all of your subordinates fairly and equally. Do not have favourites.

Steps to arbitration

As a leader you may have to adapt the role of arbitrator in conflict resolution. The conflicting parties to any dispute will have different expectations of any output, based on their values, understanding, perspective, insecurities and priorities. They will expect you as arbitrator to be impartial, fair and just.

You must prepare by carrying out the background investigation. Establish the cause of the conflict. Be open. Do not make hasty judgements. Do not take sides.

Choose a neutral location for the arbitration meeting. Sit in a central location. Try to avoid desks or tables separating the parties involved.

- Bring the conflicting parties together.
- Remain calm and professional.
- Use a common sense approach.
- Be objective.

- Deal with facts, not emotions.
- Give your understanding of the problem.
- Invite each side, in turn, to give their uninterrupted viewpoint.
- Listen to the each participant's viewpoint and remain open minded.
- Respect the viewpoint and recognise the needs of others.
- Respect and value differences.
- Support their needs but not their behaviour or reactions.
- Deal fairly with everyone involved.
- Clarify the position of each side
- Get to the root cause of the conflict.
- Communicate clearly the company point of view.
- Eliminate points of agreement from the dispute.
- Try to reach accommodation if possible.
- Summarise what has been agreed and any outstanding issues.
- Get the different parties to agree a common course of action.
- Kept your boss involved at every stage.
- Review your behaviour at a later stage to see if you could have handled anything differently.
- Learn from the situation.

Avoiding or ignoring conflict

The natural response of many people is to avoid a conflict situation. Sometimes this is the correct course of action. For instance a third party may be trying to cause conflict between two other parties in order to advance their own cause. By avoiding or ignoring any provocation you are not allowing the conflict to escalate.

Postponing dealing with conflict

Sometimes it is necessary to postpone dealing with conflict. This might be necessary to allow emotions to settle. Postponement may be required in order to gather all of the relevant information, such as witness statements. Only postpone action for as long as is necessary. The sooner you deal with issues the better.

Chapter 21. Managing meetings

The purpose of meetings

Meetings are held for the following purposes:

- To impart information to a group.
- To exchange ideas.
- To deal with group issues.
- To get the viewpoint of everyone involved.
- To make decisions based on the collective input of the group.
- To set common goals.
- To review projects.
- To update a group on important issues.
- To exchange information.
- To obtain feedback.

Meetings should not be a forum for talking. Their purpose is to decide on a course of action. There should be a clear objective. The purpose should be to achieve something tangible. All of the participants should understand the objective at the outset.

Decide if a meeting is necessary

Sometimes a meeting may not be necessary. If the objective is simply to brief the team, perhaps this could be done by issuing a report.

Schedule meetings in advance

You should schedule meetings in advance to ensure that all participants are free to attend. Schedule a time,

location and duration. Pick a location that will be free
from interruptions.

The agenda

The agenda should only include essential items. It
should be sequenced with essential items first. Set a
time limit for each item. Allocate additional time for
important issues.

Invite the decision makers

Only invite people who need to attend the meeting.
Each participant should have some input to the
meeting and leave with some tasks to carry out.
Consider why each person is required to attend:

- Have they got the authority to sign off on decisions?
- Have they got technical expertise?
- Have they got the responsibility?
- Have they got the resources?

Some people are only concerned with one or two
agenda items. Schedule their attendance accordingly.

Issue supporting material in advance

Ensure that people are properly briefed in advance of
the meeting. Distribute the agenda along with any
supporting information. Let people know how they
should prepare for the meeting. Issuing information in
advance allows people to read it in their own time.
This saves meeting time for the important discussion
and decision-making.

Hold the meetings at the right time

Avoid holding meetings at the beginning of the day. At this time people will be inclined to sit on and gossip. If you hold your meetings at the end of the day, people will be keen to finish up and get home.

Begin meetings on time

Always begin your meetings on time. If someone is late, do not go over the issues again for their benefit. It is their concern to be on time. Do not waste the time of everyone present by repeating what has already been covered.

Chair meetings effectively

Meetings have a purpose, which is to agree a plan of action for each item of the agenda. Make sure that participants switch off mobile phones during meetings so that you can concentrate on the business at hand without interruptions. The chairman must ensure that this happens.

The chairman should:

- Introduce any new participants.
- State the objective of the meeting and the time line.
- Go through each agenda item in turn.
- Reach decisions on each item.
- Seek agreement and ask for a vote if necessary.
- Encourage input, ideas and interaction.
- Encourage different viewpoints, but gain consensus.
- Keep the meeting under control.
- Bring people back to the agenda if they drift from the point.
- Remind compulsive talkers of the need for progress.

- Keep to the time limit for each agenda item.
- Seek clarification as required.
- Limit time spent debating less important issues.
- For each item in turn, summarise and record the decisions and actions.
- Resolve issues in preference to delaying them.
- Agree the action points, the accountability and the deadlines.
- Finish by summarising the main issues.
- Schedule the next meeting.

Stick to the agenda

Keep to the agenda. Do not introduce other issues. Do not let anyone else introduce other items. If someone brings up a separate concern that affects some of the participants let them remain behind and discuss it at the end. Do not have a section for any other business. This becomes a forum for gossip. If someone wants to discuss a separate issue insist that it is added to the agenda in advance. This restricts input to sensible issues.

Keep minutes

Keep minutes. There should be an action point for every agenda item. This should specify the required action, the deadline and the person responsible for completion of the work. You must issue the minutes promptly after each meeting. Allow enough time for people to action their points in advance of the next meeting. If you type the initials of the person responsible for each item it makes it easier for people to identify their areas of concern.

Copy interested parties, such as your boss, who may

not have been present.

Attending meetings

It is important that you conduct yourself professionally at meetings. There will often be senior managers present from your own and other departments. If you are attending as a participant at someone else's meeting make sure that you:

- Read the agenda and supporting information in advance.
- Bring along any information you were asked to provide.
- Keep your input brief, clear and to the point.
- Do not speak unless you have something worthwhile to contribute.
- Listen to the input of others before making your contribution.
- Do not raise an issue unless you are sure that you will get consent.
- Argue your case, but accept defeat gracefully if you are out voted.

Chapter 22. Decision making

As a leader you must be decisive. You must be able to assess a situation and come to the right conclusion on the best course of action. There are a number of stages in making an important decision:

- Analyse the problem.
- Identify the possible courses of action.
- Weigh up the risks involved.
- Consider the potential consequences.
- Do not make assumptions.
- Think about past experiences.
- Be systematic.
- Avoid procrastination.
- Consult with the interested parties.
- Choose a course of action.
- Decide on the time frame.
- Set goals and deadlines.
- Prioritise and delegate the tasks.
- Keep your boss informed.
- Implement the proposed solution.

Fear

Fear is a debilitating emotion. Fear leads to procrastination. It prevents us from taking the required action. It restricts growth. It inhibits development. In order to deal with fear you must first admit to it and then discover the underlying causes.

How many times have you worried about a situation or task and then found out it was not as daunting as first anticipated? You end up wondering what all the fuss was about. Most of our fears are completely unfounded. They are the result of negative conditioning. Fear is a negative emotion that blocks the flow of potential. Fear can manifest itself in a number of ways among your team.

- Fear of failure.
- Fear of taking risks.
- Fear of rejection.
- Fear of the unknown.
- Fear of success.
- Fear of public speaking
- Fear of speaking to senior managers.
- Fear on conveying negative news.

Overcoming procrastination

If a task seems particularly daunting and you are tempted to put it off consider the following methods of avoiding procrastination:

- List the consequences of not doing the work.
- Break a difficult task down to a series of easier tasks.
- Complete each task separately.
- If the first task seems difficult, start with an easier task.
- Delegate the parts you find difficult.
- Think about how you will feel when you have finished the task.
- Commit to the task.
- Do not wait until you feel like it.
- Reward yourself for reaching each target.

Chapter 23. Stress management

Your responsibility to your team

Stress is the contributing factor in over 13 million work days lost each year in the UK. As a leader you must be aware of the potential dangers of stress in yourself and your team. You must understand the factors that contribute to stress. You must be able to notice the early signs of stress in yourself and others. You must be able to ensure that the working environment that you manage is as free from stress as you can make it.

Understanding what stress is

Stress occurs when people experience more pressure or emotional demands than they can handle.
An acceptable level of pressure creates a challenging environment in which people can often flourish. Many people find it stimulating and motivating. However excessive pressure can lead to stress and a decline in employee performance. Excessive stress can lead to health issues and absence from work for prolonged periods.

People react to pressure in different ways. What is a perfectly acceptable challenge for one person may lead to a feeling of stress in another. Some people are more susceptible to stress than others. This may be due to differences in general health and well being levels, personality, emotional stability, self-belief and culture. Others have a better coping mechanism.

Stress induces physiological change

Stress induces physiological change in people. This helps them to cope with the situation. In the short term people get an adrenaline rush. They experience the fight or flight response. Their bodies return to normal when the reason for the stress is removed.

Longer term exposure to stress stimulates the nervous, endocrine, and immune systems. This can have a detrimental effect on health.

Causes of stress in the workplace

Stress is caused by a number of factors:

Stress induced by the working environment

- Excessive workload.
- Tight deadlines.
- Poor working conditions.
- Lack of adequate resources.
- Demotion.
- Job insecurity.

Stress induced by others

- Difficult bosses.
- Conflict with work colleagues, customers, clients or subordinates.
- Bullying or harassment.
- Conflict of demands.
- Poor communication.
- Lack of management support.
- Poor wage structure.
- Poor instructions or direction.

- Confusion over job responsibilities.

Stress induced by ourselves

- Expecting or seeking perfection.
- Poor work-life balance.
- Perceived inequality of treatment.
- Not feeling appreciated.
- Feeling inadequate.

Major life events

- Bereavement.
- Marriage.
- Divorce.
- Birth of a child.
- Moving house.
- Ill health.
- Financial concerns.

Symptoms of stress

Stress can manifest itself in many ways, depending on the individual affected. There are a variety of physical, emotional, behavioural or mental symptoms which can have a detrimental effect on work performance. They can also cause long term health issues.

Physical symptoms include tiredness, lethargy, headaches, insomnia and digestive problems.

Mental symptoms include loss of concentration, reduced attention span, slower responses, poor judgement, excessive worry and difficulty sleeping.

Behavioural symptoms include withdrawal, apathy,

aggression, emotional outbursts, over reacting, unpredictable or irrational behaviour and cynicism. Behavioural symptoms can also include loss of appetite, over eating, excessive drinking or smoking and poor work performance.

Emotional symptoms include mood swings, irritability, depression, frustration, impatience and anxiety. Emotional symptoms can also include bad temper, nervous exhaustion, panic attacks and irrational fears.

Reducing stress levels in your team

You will help to get the best out of your team if you endeavour to reduce the stress levels in their working environment. As a leader you can do this by:

- Specifying and clarifying roles.
- Setting reasonable and achievable objectives.
- Checking for the symptoms of stress in your subordinates.
- Communicating effectively.
- Tailoring your demands on people according to their abilities and capacities
- Acting on the concerns of your staff.
- Dealing promptly and firmly with conflict.
- Providing flexible working arrangements.
- Ensuring that your team takes adequate breaks.

Reducing your own stress levels at work

You must deal with stress as soon as you are aware of its presence. Otherwise it can have an adverse affect on your health. Do not deny the stress. Do not ignore the stress. Deal with it by removing the causes of the stress.

- Identify the underlying cause.
- Remove the root cause of the stress.
- Analyse why you react the way you do.
- Review excessive workload with your boss.
- Delegate as much as possible.
- Manage your time effectively.
- Prioritise your work.
- Organize your workplace.
- Learn to say no.
- Make decisions promptly.
- Be realistic about the standard of work required.
- Schedule non urgent work to be completed at a later date.
- Do not worry about things outside your remit.
- Take regular short breaks away from your office.

Establish and maintain a support network

- Discuss your concerns with friends or colleagues.
- Get help when the workload is excessive.
- End destructive relationships.
- Seek professional help if required.

Develop the correct work-life balance

- Refrain from working excessive hours.
- Do not take work home with you.
- Take regular physical exercise.
- Relax from time to time with family and friends.
- Follow a healthy, balanced diet.
- Refrain from excessive alcohol intake.
- Stop smoking.
- Meditate.
- Take up a hobby.

Chapter 24. Managing your boss

Study your boss

In order for you to be successful in your role as a leader you must be able to establish a good working relationship with your boss.

Consider your boss's management style. Think about how he prefers to get things done. Does he give clear instructions? Is he consistent in his demands? Does he tend to micromanage? Does he procrastinate? Does he make it difficult to contact him when you need him to authorise decisions? Is he making things more difficult than they really need to be? What is your boss's view of the organisation? What are the things that he thinks should be fixed? What things would he rather see carried out differently?

Establish your role

Agree with your boss on what he expects from your current position. Agree a list of short and medium term goals.

- Agree the overall targets and priorities.
- Agree on the level of your authority.
- Agree on critical deadlines.
- Agree on core activities.
- Agree on resources.
- Agree on a method of performance appraisal.

Then beat all the targets that he has set. Take on additional responsibilities. Impress your boss with your level of performance.

Agree methods of interfacing

Agree when and how often you will review your work with your boss. You should sit down at least once a week to review progress. This is critical to ensure that you are both working to the same agenda. You should agree on what kind of decisions will require consultation or approval from your boss.

You need to work with and support your boss. You need to keep him informed of the progress of your work and any likely problems. There should be no surprises. If there are likely to be issues, let him know about them as soon as possible. Do not cover up for mistakes. Admit to your faults and learn from the situation.

Find out more about your boss

Find out more about your boss in order to build rapport. Learn about his likes and dislikes. Find out how he likes to have information presented to him. Does he prefer to receive detailed reports or summarised bullet points? How does he prefer to communicate? What is his preferred medium? Does he like you to get straight to the point or does he engage in small talk first? When is the best time to approach him with a problem? When does he not like to be interrupted?

Accept your boss for what he is. You will not be able to change him. Concentrate instead on what you can do to help him succeed. Try to minimise the problems you bring to your boss. Bring solutions when you can.

If you cannot do this at least bring suggestions.

Build rapport with your boss

Build rapport with your boss. Ask about his main interests and hobbies. Talk to him about his interests. Become a friend and confidant. Support him in his goals. Remain loyal to him.

Influencing your boss

Look at ways of improving things. Bring suggestions to your boss. Get agreement where you can. Do not push him if he is unable to deliver on certain aspects. You can always return to the subject later, when you have achieved more in the role.

Chapter 25. Performance management

Every member of your team will have different levels of skills in a variety of areas. You need to point out in advance what is expected from each member of your team. In order to manage their performance you must first measure it. You then need to compare the measured results against the expected level of performance.

Measuring individual performance

A person's performance depends on their experience, their skills and their commitment. It is their commitment that you want to measure. So you need to find a method of measuring them against their own capabilities. It is no good measuring them against the performance of someone else.

You must establish a baseline for their performance against a number of key performance indicators. You can then set a target for development and milestones to be reached along the way. You must then recognise and reward them as they reach each milestone.

Measuring group performance

It is a good idea to display group results on a prominent notice board each week. You can display results by shift and by working teams. Measure results against key performance indicators. People tend to strive towards positive results rather than avoiding negative results. You should therefore specify positive indicators rather than negative indicators. For example you would report a perfect quality rate of 99% rather than a reject rate of 1%. Do not display an individual's results on notice boards.

Use charts to monitor and track performance, so that people can see the improvements. Then reward these improvements.

Formal performance reviews

Formal performance reviews should be carried out at least once per year, but preferably every three or six months. The completed reviews will need to be returned to the human resources department so that the requirements of the Data Protection Act are met. Allow an hour to cover all aspects of the employee's performance over the last year. The meeting needs to be in private and there should be no interruptions whatsoever.

Performance reviews should provide an opportunity to:

- Recap on the constant feedback you have been giving since the last formal review.
- Give specific examples of good and poor behaviour or performance
- Agree new performance goals.
- Ensure that your priorities are the same as those of your employee.
- Agree training needs.
- Discuss career development.
- Listen to the concerns of the employee.
- Provide documentation to support the case for promotion or dismissal.

There should be no surprises or bombshells for the employee in the formal appraisal. If there are, you have not been doing your job. If their performance is poor then they should have heard this message from you regularly throughout the year. Your job as a leader is to give feedback on performance every day. While you will concentrate on praise and recognition you will also be giving constructive feedback on anything that can be improved. You have to point out regularly where things can be improved if you want to increase performance levels.

If you hit one employee with a bombshell you will not only totally demoralise that employee. Word will get out immediately and the rest of the team will lose respect for your methods.

Avoiding appraisal pitfalls

Make sure that you avoid the following common mistakes when assessing employees.

Halo effect – giving an employee a high rating in all areas because he performs well in one area.
Recency effect – judging an employee's annual performance on one recent major result, either good or bad.
Mirroring - judging someone on how much they behave like you do yourself.
Comparison - judging people on how well they perform in relation to someone else.
Prejudice - judging people based on your own beliefs and concepts of stereotypes.
Bottling it – just marking everybody high so that you can avoid the negative reactions that bad news on poor performance will bring.

Disciplining

No matter how well you communicate with and lead others, there will always be people who do not share your views on the company objectives and hold your level of enthusiasm for their work. Some people will consistently underperform despite all the encouragement you give them. In this situation you will have to deal with their lack of performance. If you do not, it will affect the performance of the rest of the team. The good performers will want to know why they should put in all of the effort while someone else can get away with doing as little as possible.

Dealing with disciplinary problems

- Deal with problems promptly, before they escalate.
- Do not ignore or deny problems.
- Deal with any personnel issues in private.
- If there has been conflict do not take sides.
- Look for the underlying causes.
- Separate the performance issue from the person.
- Describe the problem without evaluating the behaviour.
- Describe the effect of their behaviour on the team.
- Ask for an explanation.
- Do not comment on the attitude of the person.
- Consider mitigating circumstances.
- Explain the required behaviour.
- Give a time-line for improvement.
- Consider the needs of the wider team.
- Be prepared to cut your losses if required.

Discipline should be used to tackle problems promptly before they become a major concern. The aim is to improve performance rather than to punish.

Disciplinary procedures

Each organisation has their own disciplinary procedures and as a leader you will be expected to follow these when dealing with either poor performance or cases of misconduct. The whole purpose of having disciplinary procedures is that everyone is dealt with in the same manner. This should happen regardless of position, occupation or length of service. Part time and temporary employees have the same rights as full time employees.

The golden rule is to involve the Human Resources department before you take any action. Follow their guidelines on:

- Carrying out a thorough investigation in advance.
- Taking any witness statements.
- Determining if disciplinary action might be appropriate.
- Timing and method of informing the employee of the disciplinary action.
- Notification of representation that the employee is entitled to.
- Location and date of disciplinary meeting and necessary attendants.
- Giving an opportunity for the employee to defend his case.
- Disciplinary paperwork that needs to be completed, signed and witnessed.
- Level of warning that is appropriate.
- Length of time warning remains on the employee's file.
- Follow up and review required.
- Appeal procedures.

Conducting a disciplinary hearing

When conducting a disciplinary hearing you should have someone to take notes on the proper company disciplinary interview sheets. You need to specify exactly what the unacceptable behaviour was. Relate the behaviour to specific performance standards that were not met or specific policies that they were in breach of. You need to ask the employee for their view of the events and the reason for their behaviour. You need to probe for and take into account any mitigating circumstances. You must take into account their previous record. You must explain the impact of the behaviour on others.

You must outline the desired standard of behaviour that they must achieve in line with company standards or policies. You must explain the next stage of disciplinary action that will occur if the desired improvement in behaviour does not materialise. Ask if there is anything that you can do to support the employee in improving their behaviour. Provide a performance improvement plan that will help the employee to reach his targets. The improvement plan will include a goal, a schedule and any supporting resources.

Progressive approach to disciplining

Most companies will have a sliding scale of warnings. First time, minor infringements may only get an informal verbal admonishment from the immediate supervisor that is not strictly part of the documented process. If you issue an informal verbal warning make sure that you record it in your diary. You may wish to send a note to the personnel department as well. On the next occasion an employee would receive a verbal warning which is recorded on their record. A third transgression would involve a written warning being issued. If a fourth problem occurs the employee would be issued with a final written warning. Any further problems could lead to dismissal. There will be a recommended time limit that a warning would remain on someone's record before it expires. With many companies higher level warnings will stay longer on an employee's file.

Mitigating or contributing circumstances

Your job as a leader is to discipline employees who continually fail to reach performance targets. If there are any mitigating or contributing circumstances then you need to get the appropriate expert intervention. An employee may have a dependency or health issue. In this case you would discuss the issue with the human resources department and have them referred to the company doctor.

Someone may have problems outside of work. Perhaps they are not getting any sleep due to a new baby having been born. In this case you may be able to be flexible on working patterns rather than dealing with a time keeping problem.

Transferring an employee

Sometimes an employee is promoted to a level beyond their capability. If the employee has been in a previous job within the company where their performance was acceptable you may consider moving them to another less demanding role. You will probably need to get the agreement of your boss and the human resources department before carrying out this move. The move may involve a lower salary and could well involve a period of probation. The employee will have to sign off their agreement to these terms.

Misconduct

Misconduct is usually considered a more serious problem that lack of performance. The company terms and conditions booklet will have a section which outlines the different forms and levels of misconduct. Minor misconduct may be subject to a written warning while gross misconduct may lead to immediate suspension and a disciplinary hearing that could lead to dismissal if the case is proved. Examples of gross misconduct are theft, physically attacking another employee and being under the influence of alcohol or drugs.

Chapter 26. Networking

No one is an island

We are all social animals. No one is an island. We need the help and encouragement of others.
We can achieve more through the help and intercession of others than we can ever hope to achieve in isolation.

Surround yourself with the best people

Surround yourself with the best people. Hire skilled, ambitious people who have the right attitude. Seek alliances with people within your company who share your values and can help you to get things done.

Get involved

Get involved in work charity events and outings. It is a great way to interact socially with others and build friendships.

Avoid negative people

Avoid negative people and those who indulge in gossip and rumour spreading. You will be judged by association if you spend time with this type of person.

Social networks

You can connect with people with similar interests and concerns through LinkedIn or Facebook groups.

Chapter 27. Change management

Change management

Companies need to be constantly changing and developing in order to survive. They need to react to changes in demand by developing new products, new processes and new methods of trading. There is a need for process improvements to improve quality and reduce costs in order to remain competitive. Companies who welcome and embrace change are more likely to succeed in the long run.

Implementing change requires commitment from the top of the organisation. The most important aspect of change management is to achieve commitment to change amongst employees. Employers expect their employees to be flexible to change. They need their employees to be willing to alter their duties, working patterns and workloads depending on changing patterns of demand. The best way to do this is to create a working environment that is conducive to change. Such an environment will stress the importance of education, learning, training and development of the workforce.

External Triggers to change:

There are many external triggers to change, including:

- The need to improve operations.
- Competitor action.
- Customer requests.
- Market opportunities.

- Changes in demand.
- Changes in value.
- Changing technology.
- Changes in regulation or legislation.
- Environmental issues.
- Acquisitions and mergers.

Internal triggers to change

- Company vision and strategy.
- Pricing policy.
- Corporate restructuring.
- Changes in management.
- Company expansion or contraction.
- The need to improve morale.
- The need to reduce turnover.

Implementing change successfully

The first stage of managing change is to identify the stakeholders. Who will be affected by the change? Who needs to implement the change? These people must be identified and the change needs to be communicated to them as early as possible. Reasons for the change need to be explained. The outcome of the change needs to be explained along with the perceived benefits. This will help people prepare for the change and overcome any fears and objections.

You must be truthful with people when communicating change. You should involve people in the decision making process as much as possible. If people are given a degree of ownership they are more likely to support any change. If it is imposed on them without consultation they are more likely to resist the change, either actively or passively.

Take the following steps when implementing change:

- Communicate the change in advance.
- Justify the change.
- Explain the reasons.
- Explain how the company will benefit from the change.
- Explain the method of implementation, the timing and the likely disruption.
- Explain to everyone how they will be affected by the change.
- Provide a motive for change.
- Identify key personnel to drive through the change.
- Prepare a plan to implement the change.
- Encourage participation, invite questions, listen to feedback and act on it.
- Give employees time to get used to the idea of change.
- Involve people in the decision making.
- Carry out any required training.
- Implement the change.
- Monitor the implementation and get feedback.
- Provide support with new procedures.
- Review the outcome of the change.

Be aware that the change may benefit the organisation as a whole, but it may actually be detrimental to some members of your team. If this is the case you will have to take additional time to explain the necessity of the change.

Company expectation of employee attitude to change

Most companies expect their leaders and employees to

welcome change. They expect that leaders and their teams will:

- Be dissatisfied with the current status.
- Continually question how things are done.
- Be flexible and welcome change.
- Seek to learn new skills
- Adapt to circumstances.
- Recognise that change is inevitable.
- Maintain a positive attitude.
- View change as an opportunity.
- Be proactive in bringing change about.

You must be prepared to promote and implement change in your role as a leader.

Actual employee attitude to change

How employees actually react to change is dramatically different from how most organisations would like them to feel about it. One of the biggest challenges a leader can face is to lead his team through organisational change. Many people are uncomfortable with change. They will tend to resist it. They prefer not to encounter change. It disrupts their sense of continuity. They would rather remain within their comfort zones. People do not like change that is imposed on them. They feel that this causes them to lose control. They may have to learn new skills. They go from being a skilled worker one day, to feeling like an over aged trainee the next day.

Change can also mean having to join a new team, reporting to a new boss and relocating within the company. This is all very well when the employee has applied for a different role. It is another matter all together when the change is being enforced by the company.

Job security

People tend to be anxious about how change might affect their job security. Any hint of change in a workplace will automatically set the rumour mill going. This is why it is important to communicate change as soon as possible. Change must be communicated at every level and to everyone affected by the change. This must be done face to face. Any void in information will be filled with speculation and rumour.

Resistance to operational change

Resistance to operational change occurs when it is seen as a threat to current terms or conditions. The resistance will be highest amongst the personnel who feel that they have the most to lose. Change can lead to fear, uncertainty and doubt. People generally prefer the familiarity and security of what they have become accustomed to. The do not like the perceived risk involved with change. What people do not know they fear. What they fear they fight or resist. Many of the concerns involve:

- The change of role.
- The change of routine.
- Loss of control.
- Fear of the unknown.
- Fear of failure.
- Implied criticism of current methods.
- Fear of losing position, power or status.
- Working for a new boss.

- Joining a new team.
- Working in a new area.
- Changes to terms and conditions.
- Additional duties.
- Dislike of the methods used to introduce change.
- Feeling of interference in their work environment.
- Moving from being an experienced employee to uncertainty in their role.

Active resistance

Resistance to change may be active or passive. If the resistance is active the person will voice concerns. This helps in that the resistance is out in the open and can be dealt with. Ask probing questions to ascertain exactly what it is that the person is objecting to. What is his main concerns and fears. Then use persuasion and further clarification to try and influence his reaction to the change. Take into account any suggestion the person gives. If you can implement them alongside the change then you are likely to get his cooperation. As a last resort you will have to tell this person that the change must be implemented for the overall good of the organisation.

Passive resistance

Sometimes you will encounter passive resistance. This is where a person will say that they support the change, but then do nothing to help implement and work the new arrangements. In this case you may decide to give it a few days to see if they begin to appreciate the benefits. If this does not happen you need to interview the person in private and get his objections out in the open. It is only by discussing problems that they can be resolved.

Use incremental steps

To help people cope with change you should introduce it in incremental steps. Do not ask your team members to do too much at the one time. Do not overwhelm them. Do not induce stress by overloading them. Introduce the change in gradual steps. Allow them to master each stage before moving on to new challenges. Monitor the progress and provide feedback. Recognise the achievements of your team as they acquire new skills. Encourage them to continue on the journey of change. Help them overcome any problems by providing expert tuition if required.

Review the success of the change

Once the change has been implemented and had a period of time to bed down, you should assess the success or otherwise of the change. Review the improvements and look for any areas where performance has suffered. If the change has been cross departmental then hold a review meeting with other management. Take suggestions and consider any further improvements that can be made. Agree a course of action. Then repeat the whole process of communicating and implementing further change.

Continual improvement

Continual improvement needs to be part of the culture of your team. Change should be the norm rather than the exception. The key to a successful outcome is to try where possible to only change one parameter at a time and monitor the effect the change has on results. If you change more than one parameter at a time it is difficult to assess the effect of the individual changes.

Also by Terry Melaugh

Get That Job - The Ultimate Guide

http://amzn.com/B00BV74E4E

How to Succeed at Work - The Ultimate Guide by
Terry Melaugh

http://www.amazon.co.uk/dp/B00CA9YOII